Unit
Assessments

Mc
Graw
Hill
Education

mheducation.com/prek-12

Send all inquiries to:
McGraw-Hill Education
Two Penn Plaza
New York, New York 10121

ISBN: 978-0-07-901758-1
MHID: 0-07-901758-4

Printed in the United States of America.

4 5 6 7 8 LHS 24 23 22 21

A

Table of Contents

Unit Assessments

The *Unit Assessments* component is an integral part of the complete assessment program aligned with *Wonders* and state standards.

Purpose

This component reports on the outcome of student learning. As students complete each unit of the reading program, they will be assessed on their understanding of key instructional content and their ability to write to source texts/stimuli. The results serve as a summative assessment by providing a status of current achievement in relation to student progress through the curriculum. The results of the assessments can be used to inform subsequent instruction, aid in making leveling and grouping decisions, and point toward areas in need of reteaching or remediation.

Focus

Unit Assessments focuses on key areas of English Language Arts—comprehension of literature and informational text, vocabulary acquisition and use, command of the conventions of the English language, and genre writing in response to sources.

Each unit assessment also provides students familiarity with the item types, the test approaches, and the increased rigor associated with the advances in state-mandated high-stakes assessments.

Test Administration

Each unit assessment should be administered once the instruction for the specific unit is completed. Make copies of the unit assessment for the class. You will need copies of the answer key pages that feature the scoring charts for each student taking the assessment, which provide a place to list student scores. The data from each unit assessment charts student progress and underscores strengths and weaknesses.

This component is the pencil-and-paper version of the assessment. You can administer the online version of the test, which allows for technology-enhanced item functionality.

NOTE: Due to time constraints, you may wish to administer the unit assessment over multiple days. For example, students can complete the 20-item test on the first day and complete the performance task on another. For planning purposes, the recommended time for each performance task is 90–100 minutes over two back-to-back sessions. During the first session, provide students 30–40 minutes to read the stimulus materials and answer the research questions. During the second session, provide students 60–70 minutes for planning, writing, and editing their responses. If desired, provide students a short break between sessions. If you decide to break-up administration by assessment sections, please remember to withhold those sections of the test students are not completing to ensure test validity.

After each student has a copy of the assessment, provide a version of the following directions:

Teacher Introduction

Say: *Write your name on the question pages for this assessment.* (When students are finished, continue with the directions.) *You will read three texts and answer questions about them. In the next part of the test, you will read a student draft that you will revise or edit for the correct grammar, mechanics, and usage. In the final part of the test, you will read sources, answer questions about them, and write a response based on the assignment you will find, which will ask you to use those sources in your writing.*

Read each part of the test carefully. For multiple-choice items, circle the letter next to the correct answer or answers. For other types of questions, look carefully at the directions. You may be asked to match items, circle or underline choices, or complete a chart. For the constructed-response question, write your response on the lines provided. For the performance task, write your response to the assignment on separate sheets of paper. When you have completed the assessment, put your pencil down and turn the pages over. You may begin now.

Answer procedural questions during the assessment, but do not provide any assistance on the items or selections. Have extra paper on hand for students to use for their performance task responses. After the class has completed the assessment, ask students to verify that their names are written on the necessary pages.

Assessment Items

Unit assessments feature the following item types—selected response (SR), multiple selected response (MSR), evidence-based selected response (EBSR), constructed response (CR), and technology-enhanced items (TE). (Please note that the print versions of TE items are available in this component; the full functionality of the items is available only through the online assessment.) This variety of item types provides multiple methods of assessing student understanding, allows for deeper investigation into skills and strategies, and provides students an opportunity to become familiar with the kinds of questions they will encounter in state-mandated summative assessments.

Performance Tasks

Each unit features a performance task (PT) assessment in a previously taught genre. Students will complete two examples of each task type by the end of the year.

- Narrative
  - Students craft a narrative using information from the sources.
- Informational
  - Students generate a thesis based on the sources and use information from the sources to explain this thesis.
- Opinion
  - Students analyze the ideas in sources and make a claim that they support using the sources.

Each PT assesses standards that address comprehension, research skills, genre writing, and the use of standard English language conventions (ELC). The stimulus texts and research questions in each task build toward the goal of the final writing topic.

Overview

- Students will read three texts in each assessment and respond to items focusing on comprehension skills, literary elements, text features, and vocabulary strategies. These items assess the ability to access meaning from the text and demonstrate understanding of unknown and multiple-meaning words and phrases.

- Students will then read a student draft that requires corrections or clarifications to its use of the conventions of standard English language or complete a cloze passage that requires correct usage identification.

- Students are then presented with a performance task assessment.

Each test item in *Unit Assessments* (as well as in progress monitoring and benchmark assessments) has a Depth of Knowledge (DOK) level assigned to it.

Vocabulary items

DOK 1: Use word parts (affixes, roots) to determine the meaning of an unknown word.

DOK 2: Use context or print/digital resources to determine the meaning of an unknown or multiple-meaning word; use context to understand figurative language.

Comprehension items

DOK 1: Identify/locate information in the text.

DOK 2: Analyze text structures/literary elements.

DOK 3: Make inferences using text evidence and analyze author's craft.

DOK 4: Respond using multiple texts.

Revising and Editing items

DOK 1: Edit to fix errors

DOK 2: Revise for clarity and coherence.

Each unit assessment features three "cold reads" on which the comprehension and vocabulary assessment items are based. These selections reflect the unit theme and genre-studies to support the focus of the classroom instruction. Texts fall within the Lexile band 520L–820L. Complexity on this quantitative measure grows throughout the units, unless a qualitative measure supports text placement outside a lockstep Lexile continuum.

Comprehension

Comprehension items assess student understanding of the text through the use of the comprehension skills, literary elements, and text features taught throughout the unit.

Vocabulary

Vocabulary items ask students to demonstrate their ability to uncover the meanings of unknown and multiple-meaning words and phrases using vocabulary strategies.

English Language Conventions

Five items in each unit ask students to demonstrate their command of the conventions of standard English.

Performance Task

Students complete one performance task per unit, which includes research questions and a final written response in the specified task genre.

Scoring

Each unit assessment totals 35 points. Comprehension and vocabulary items are worth two points each. Constructed-response and multi-part items should be answered correctly in full, though you may choose to provide partial credit. Revising and editing items are worth one point each. Use the scoring chart at the bottom of the answer key to record each student's score. Note that the performance task is scored separately, as described below.

For the constructed-response items, assign a score using the correct response parameters provided in the answer key along with the scoring rubrics shown below. Responses that show a complete lack of understanding or are left blank should be given a *0*.

Short Response Score 2: The response is well-crafted and concise and shows a thorough understanding of the underlying skill. Appropriate text evidence is used to answer the question.

Short Response Score 1: The response shows partial understanding of the underlying skill. Text evidence is featured, though examples are too general.

Each unit performance task is a separate 15-point assessment. The three research items are worth a total of five points, broken down as indicated in the scoring charts. Score the written response holistically on a 10-point scale, using the rubrics on the following pages:

- 4 points for purpose/organization [P/O]

- 4 points for evidence/elaboration [E/E] or development/elaboration [D/E]

- 2 points for English language conventions [C]

- Unscorable or 0-point responses are unrelated to the topic, illegible, contain little or no writing, or show little to no command of the conventions of standard English.

Use the top-score anchor paper response provided in the answer key for each test for additional scoring guidance.

Teacher Introduction

NARRATIVE PERFORMANCE TASK SCORING RUBRIC

Score	Purpose/Organization	Development/Elaboration	Conventions
4	• **fully sustained** organization; **clear** focus • effective, unified plot • effective development of setting, characters, point of view • transitions clarify relationships between and among ideas • logical sequence of events • effective opening and closing	• **effective** elaboration with details, dialogue, description • clear expression of experiences and events • effective use of relevant source material • effective use of various narrative techniques • effective use of sensory, concrete, and figurative language	
3	• **adequately sustained** organization; **generally maintained** focus • evident plot with loose connections • adequate development of setting, characters, point of view • adequate use of transitional strategies • adequate sequence of events • adequate opening and closing	• **adequate** elaboration with details, dialogue, description • adequate expression of experiences and events • adequate use of source material • adequate use of various narrative techniques • adequate use of sensory, concrete, and figurative language	
2	• **somewhat sustained** organization; **uneven** focus • inconsistent plot with evident flaws • uneven development of setting, characters, point of view • uneven use of transitional strategies, with little variety • weak or uneven sequence of events • weak opening and closing	• **uneven** elaboration with **partial** details, dialogue, description • uneven expression of experiences and events • vague, abrupt, or imprecise use of source material • uneven, inconsistent use of narrative technique • partial or weak use of sensory, concrete, and figurative language	• **adequate** command of spelling, capitalization, punctuation, grammar, and usage • few errors
1	• **basic** organization; **little or no** focus • little or no discernible plot; may just be a series of events • brief or no development of setting, characters, point of view • few or no transitional strategies • little or no organization of event sequence; extraneous ideas • no opening and/or closing	• **minimal** elaboration with **few or no** details, dialogue, description • confusing expression of experiences and events • little or no use of source material • minimal or incorrect use of narrative techniques • little or no use of sensory, concrete, and figurative language	• **partial** command of spelling, capitalization, punctuation, grammar, and usage • some patterns of errors

Unit Assessments

INFORMATIONAL PERFORMANCE TASK SCORING RUBRIC

Score	Purpose/Organization	Evidence/Elaboration	Conventions
4	• **effective** organizational structure • clear statement of main idea based on purpose, audience, task • consistent use of various transitions • logical progression of ideas	• **convincing** support for main idea; **effective** use of sources • integrates comprehensive evidence from sources • relevant references • effective use of elaboration • audience-appropriate domain-specific vocabulary	
3	• **evident** organizational structure • adequate statement of main idea based on purpose, audience, task • adequate, somewhat varied use of transitions • adequate progression of ideas	• **adequate** support for main idea; **adequate** use of sources • some integration of evidence from sources • references may be general • adequate use of some elaboration • generally audience-appropriate domain-specific vocabulary	
2	• **inconsistent** organizational structure • unclear or somewhat unfocused main idea • inconsistent use of transitions with little variety • formulaic or uneven progression of ideas	• **uneven** support for main idea; **limited** use of sources • weakly integrated, vague, or imprecise evidence from sources • references are vague or absent • weak or uneven elaboration • uneven domain-specific vocabulary	• **adequate** command of spelling, capitalization, punctuation, grammar, and usage • few errors
1	• **little or no** organizational structure • few or no transitions • frequent extraneous ideas; may be formulaic • may lack introduction and/or conclusion • confusing or ambiguous focus; may be very brief	• **minimal** support for main idea; **little or no** use of sources • minimal, absent, incorrect, or irrelevant evidence from sources • references are absent or incorrect • minimal, if any, elaboration • limited or ineffective domain-specific vocabulary	• **partial** command of spelling, capitalization, punctuation, grammar, and usage • some patterns of errors

OPINION PERFORMANCE TASK SCORING RUBRIC

Score	Purpose/Organization	Evidence/Elaboration	Conventions
4	• **effective** organizational structure; **sustained** focus • consistent use of various transitions • logical progression of ideas • effective introduction and conclusion • clearly communicated opinion for purpose, audience, task	• **convincing** support/evidence for main idea; **effective** use of sources; **precise** language • comprehensive evidence from sources is integrated • relevant, specific references • effective elaborative techniques • appropriate domain-specific vocabulary for audience, purpose	
3	• **evident** organizational structure; **adequate** focus • adequate use of transitions • adequate progression of ideas • adequate introduction and conclusion • clear opinion, mostly maintained, though loosely • adequate opinion for purpose, audience, task	• **adequate** support/evidence for main idea; **adequate** use of sources; **general** language • some evidence from sources is integrated • general, imprecise references • adequate elaboration • generally appropriate domain-specific vocabulary for audience, purpose	
2	• **inconsistent** organizational structure; **somewhat sustained** focus • inconsistent use of transitions • uneven progression of ideas • introduction or conclusion, if present, may be weak • somewhat unclear or unfocused opinion	• **uneven** support for main idea; **partial** use of sources; **simple** language • evidence from sources is weakly integrated, vague, or imprecise • vague, unclear references • weak or uneven elaboration • uneven or somewhat ineffective use of domain-specific vocabulary for audience, purpose	• **adequate** command of spelling, capitalization, punctuation, grammar, and usage • few errors
1	• **little or no** organizational structure or focus • few or no transitions • frequent extraneous ideas are evident; may be formulaic • introduction and/or conclusion may be missing • confusing opinion	• **minimal** support for main idea; **little or no** use of sources; **vague** language • source material evidence is minimal, incorrect, or irrelevant • references absent or incorrect • minimal, if any, elaboration • limited or ineffective use of domain-specific vocabulary for audience, purpose	• **partial** command of spelling, capitalization, punctuation, grammar, and usage • some patterns of errors

Evaluating Scores

The answer keys have been constructed to provide the information you need to aid your understanding of student performance, as well as individualized instructional and intervention needs.

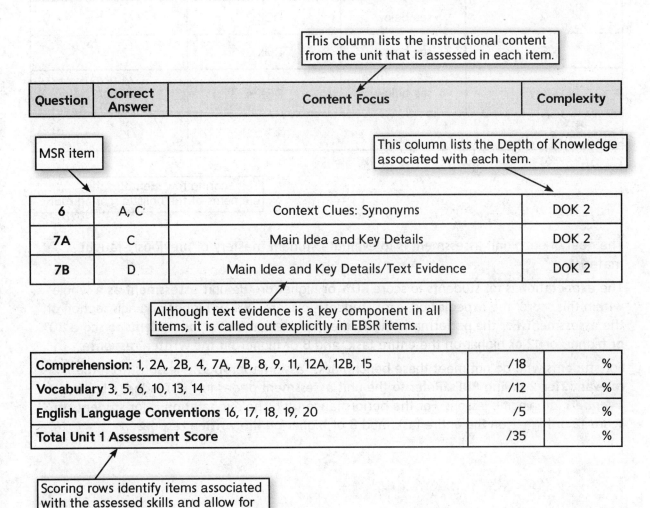

This column lists the instructional content from the unit that is assessed in each item.

Question	Correct Answer	Content Focus	Complexity

This column lists the Depth of Knowledge associated with each item.

MSR item

Question	Correct Answer	Content Focus	Complexity
6	A, C	Context Clues: Synonyms	DOK 2
7A	C	Main Idea and Key Details	DOK 2
7B	D	Main Idea and Key Details/Text Evidence	DOK 2

Although text evidence is a key component in all items, it is called out explicitly in EBSR items.

Comprehension: 1, 2A, 2B, 4, 7A, 7B, 8, 9, 11, 12A, 12B, 15	/18	%
Vocabulary 3, 5, 6, 10, 13, 14	/12	%
English Language Conventions 16, 17, 18, 19, 20	/5	%
Total Unit 1 Assessment Score	/35	%

Scoring rows identify items associated with the assessed skills and allow for quick record keeping.

Teacher Introduction

Narrative Performance Task			
Question	**Answer**	**Complexity**	**Score**
1	see below	DOK 2	/1
2	see below	DOK 3	/2
3	see below	DOK 3	/2
Story	see below	DOK 4	/4 [P/O] /4 [D/E] /2 [C]
Total Score			**/15**

This scoring row identifies the elements of the holistic scoring rubric.

The goal of each unit assessment is to evaluate student mastery of previously-taught material.

The expectation is for students to score 80% or higher on the unit assessment as a whole; within this score, the expectation is for students to score 75% or higher on each section of the assessment. For the performance task, the expectation also is for students to score 80% or higher, or 12 or higher on the entire task, and 8 or higher on the written response.

For students who do not meet these benchmarks, assign appropriate lessons from the relevant **Tier 2 online PDFs**. Refer to the unit assessment pages in the Teacher's Edition of *Wonders* for specific lessons. For the performance task, the expectation is for students to score 12 or higher on the entire task, and 8 or higher on the written response.

Read the passage. Then answer the questions.

New Kid in School

Jayden watched the kids play from his corner of the school playground. Some were swinging on the swings or sliding down the slide. Others were kicking a dirty old soccer ball around. It was his third day at his new school and his third recess period standing in the corner of the playground, alone. He wished someone would ask him to swing, slide, or play soccer, but no one did. That day after school, Jayden walked home slowly with his head down. As he passed the park, shouting and laughing caught his attention.

"Over here!" someone shouted. "Kick it! Kick it to me!" somebody hollered. It was some neighborhood kids playing soccer. Jayden stopped to watch them and recognized several of his classmates. He paused a few minutes to observe them. He was hoping they would see him and invite him to join their game, but no one did.

Jayden missed his old school and his old friends. "Why did we have to move?" he muttered to himself under his breath. "I don't have any friends here. I'll never have any friends here. Back home, I had Shawn, Jorge, and Nora. Back home, I—" Jayden caught himself. This was his home now, whether he liked it or not.

When he reached his house, it appeared empty. "Mom?" he called out, walking from room to room. "Mom? I'm home." Then he noticed a note attached to the refrigerator. It read: "Barry and I are across the street at our neighbor's house. Come on over, honey."

In the neighbor's backyard, Jayden saw his mother talking with a woman. They were chatting over cups of tea at a patio table. His three-year-old brother Barry and a little girl about the same age were playing in a sandbox.

"Hi, sweetie!" his mother called. "How was school today?"

"Okay," Jayden replied, though it hadn't been.

GO ON →

"This is our neighbor, Mrs. Ori, and her little girl Ava."

Just then, Ava reached out and grabbed the toy car at Barry's feet.

"Uh-oh," Jayden thought. "Look out!"

The car was Barry's favorite toy, and if anybody else touched it, he would wail and cry and kick. But this time, the wail and the kicks didn't happen. Instead, Barry watched Ava roll the car through the sand. Then he picked up a toy truck and did the same.

That night in bed, Jayden did some thinking. "Maybe I've been going at this friends business the wrong way. I've been waiting for people to make friends with me. Maybe I should try to make friends with them," he said to himself. The next day on the playground, he approached Tyler, one of the soccer players he'd seen the day before.

"Hi," Jayden smiled. "I got this new soccer ball for my birthday a few weeks ago. Do you want to use it instead of that old mushy one?"

"Sure!" Tyler answered. "Do you want to be on my side? What position do you play?"

Out loud, Jayden said, "I play forward." To himself, he said, "Who ever thought I could learn something from my three-year-old brother!"

GO ON →

1   What happens first in the passage?

   A Jayden sees kids playing soccer in the park.

   B Jayden watches classmates in the playground.

   C Jayden goes to his neighbor's backyard.

   D Jayden walks home from school.

2   The following question has two parts. First, answer part A. Then, answer part B.

Part A: When does Jayden begin to realize his mistake?

   A when he thinks about how Barry plays with Ava

   B when he sees the note his mother leaves him

   C when he is introduced to his new neighbor

   D when he offers his soccer ball to Tyler

Part B: Which sentence from the passage **best** supports the answer in part A?

   A "It was some neighborhood kids playing soccer."

   B "He was hoping they would see him and invite him to join their game, but no one did."

   C "Then he noticed a note attached to the refrigerator."

   D "To himself, he said, 'Who ever thought I could learn something from my three-year-old brother!'"

GO ON →

3   Read the sentence from the passage.

Instead, Barry watched Ava <u>roll</u> the car through the sand.

What is the meaning of the word <u>roll</u> in the sentence?

   A a type of bread

   B the sound of a drum

   C to turn over and over

   D to move using wheels

4   Which words **best** describe Jayden at the end of the passage? Pick **two** choices.

   A embarrassed

   B confused

   C excited

   D tired

   E angry

   F hopeful

5   Circle the compound word in the paragraph below.

"Hi," Jayden smiled. "I got this new soccer ball for my birthday a few

weeks ago. Do you want to use it instead of that old mushy one?"

GO ON →

Read the passage. Then answer the questions.

A Gulf Coast Rescue

Somewhere off the coast of Louisiana, a small motor raft cruises along slowly. On a normal summer day, the water would be filled with boats. Jet skis would zoom by. Sailboats would glide with the wind. Happy faces would smile. But not in July of 2010.

The little raft turns into Barataria Bay and starts to inch along the coast. Volunteers stand at watch and point to the water when they see something. The little raft stops, and someone scoops a brown pelican out of the water with a net.

The bird is like many other animals here in the bay. It is covered in a layer of oil. The sludge is visible to the rescuers. Below the surface, sea turtles, dolphins, and other animals are also covered. What has happened? To understand, we must go back in time three months.

In the Gulf of Mexico, deep-water oil wells exist. Oil companies have built these wells to help them pump oil from the ocean floor. On April 20, 2010, one of the wells exploded. Oil from the damaged well began flowing into the Gulf. For three long months, the oil company struggled to find ways to plug the flow of oil. But an ugly stain of floating oil began to grow. It spread each day, and before long, the oil started to wash up on the Gulf's beaches. By the time the well was shut down, the damage was done. By then, almost five million barrels of oil had spilled into the Gulf.

The oil affected the animals. It polluted the seawater. It destroyed grasses and plants along the shore that animals needed for food and shelter. People knew they had to work fast to save as many animals as they could. There was no time to waste! Quickly, rescue centers began to dot the shoreline, and boats set out to find and rescue those in trouble.

GO ON →

Meanwhile, the volunteers in the little raft arrive at shore with the pelican in distress. Rescuers give the bird food and water. They are careful with it. The pelican is not used to being handled by people. There are many other animals at the rescue center, mostly birds and sea turtles.

Once the pelican's needs are met, the rescuers gently clean it with warm water and dish soap before rinsing. Afterwards, it is left alone to rest and dry off before joining other cleaned animals. Most will stay at the rescue center for a few days or weeks. They are watched very carefully. When rescuers are sure that an animal is healthy, they release it back into the wild in areas that have also been cleaned.

It is hard to know what will happen next. But rescue volunteers are trying to help. It is all they can do. The little raft goes out to Barataria Bay to search again. It will continue searching until there are no animals left to help.

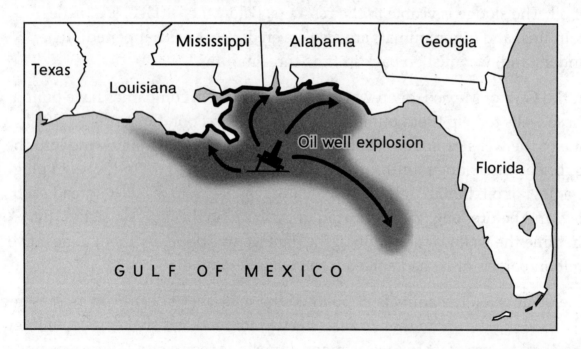

GO ON →

6   Read the sentence from the passage.

The <u>sludge</u> is visible to the rescuers.

What does the word <u>sludge</u> mean? Pick **two** choices.

A   dirty mixture

B   soapy water

C   slimy mud

D   feathers

E   weeds

7   The following question has two parts. First, answer part A. Then, answer part B.

Part A: What is the main idea of the passage?

A   An oil company tries to stop the flow of oil in the Gulf.

B   Volunteers must work quickly to save a pelican that is covered in oil.

C   Rescue workers try to help animals after an oil spill occurs in the Gulf.

D   Birds, sea turtles, and dolphins live near an oil well.

Part B: Which sentence from the passage **best** supports the answer in Part A?

A   "The bird is like many other animals here in the bay."

B   "In the Gulf of Mexico, deep-water oil wells exist."

C   "There are many other animals at the rescue center, mostly birds and sea turtles."

D   "It will continue searching until there are no animals left to help."

GO ON →

8 How does the map help the reader understand the information about the Gulf Coast better? Use details from the passage to support your answer.

_____

_____

_____

_____

_____

9 How is the information in the passage organized?

   A by giving a new solution to save many animals in the Gulf

   B by listing the many effects of just one volunteer in the Gulf

   C by retelling the sequence of events that took place after the Gulf oil spill

   D by comparing the Gulf oil spill to other oil spills that happened in history

GO ON →

10   Read the sentence from the passage.

Quickly, rescue centers began to dot the <u>shoreline</u>, and boats set out to find and rescue those in trouble.

What does the word <u>shoreline</u> mean?

A   the middle of the ocean

B   where the bay meets land

C   the side of a boat

D   far away from water

GO ON →

Read the passage. Then answer the questions.

Make Time for Family Time

People have busy lives. In fact, most people are so busy that it is easy to forget about some other things, like family. But family is an important part of life. The best way to show family they are important is to have family time every week.

What Is Family Time?

It is a special day or time when your family does something as a group. It can be any activity. Together, families choose what they want to do.

When Do You Do It?

It can be anytime. Some families do things at home on Friday nights. Others go out every Sunday. They often choose a time based on everyone's schedule. It doesn't matter what day or time it is, as long as families make a point to do it.

Who Is Invited?

Family is invited! The word "family" means different things to different people. Some people live with their parents, brothers, and sisters. Others live with grandparents. Some live with aunts or uncles or adopted families. All of these people are family.

Why Should You Do It?

Family time is fun, but there are other good reasons to do it, too. It helps you be close to your family members. It gives you a chance to talk with them and share your thoughts and feelings. It also helps you get to know your family better. Best of all, it gives you great memories of your time together. For these reasons and more, it's important to make time for family time!

> Here are some great ideas for family time!
> • play a board game
> • watch a movie at home
> • try a new recipe
> • go for a long walk

GO ON →

11 Complete the chart to match each detail to the heading under which it is found. Mark **one** box next to **each** detail.

	What Is Family Time?	When Do You Do It?	Who Is Invited	Why Should You Do It?
The day and time don't matter.	☐	☐	☐	☐
It creates great memories.	☐	☐	☐	☐
Families choose the activity.	☐	☐	☐	☐
Some kids live with grandparents.	☐	☐	☐	☐

12 The following question has two parts. First, answer part A. Then, answer part B.

Part A: What is the main idea of the passage?

A Family time is a good way to connect with family.

B Some people have very large extended families.

C People are too busy doing chores these days.

D Many people think spending time with family is boring.

GO ON →

Part B: Which sentence from the passage **best** supports the answer in part A?

A "In fact, most people are so busy that it is easy to forget about some other things, like family."

B "The best way to show family they are important is to have family time every week."

C "The word 'family' means different things to different people."

D "Some people live with their parents, brothers, and sisters."

13 Read the sentences from the passage.

Others go out every Sunday. They often choose a time based on everyone's <u>schedule</u>.

Which words from the sentences give a clue to the meaning of the word <u>schedule</u>? Pick **two** choices.

A "go out"

B "every Sunday"

C "often choose"

D "a time"

E "based on"

GO ON →

14   Read the sentence from the passage.

It helps you be <u>close</u> to your family members.

Which of the following **best** describes how <u>close</u> is used in the sentence?

A   in space

B   in time

C   in distance

D   in feeling

15   Look at the information in the sidebar. What heading **best** goes with the sidebar?

A   What Is Family Time?

B   When Do You Do It?

C   Who Is Invited?

D   Why Should You Do It?

GO ON →

The draft below needs revision. Read the draft. Then answer the questions.

(1) When I turned eight, I asked for a pct. (2) My parents took me to an animal shelter to choose one. (3) One large room full of barking dogs in cages. (4) Some were quiet, they all wanted new homes.

(5) Dad said, "I wonder if a dog is the best pet for us. (6) Think about it. (7) Our apartment is pretty small. (8) How would you like a cat."

(9) The cat room was full, too. (10) In one cage was a pile of sleeping kittens. (11) In the next cage, an older cat was taking a nap. (12) Then I saw two orange and white cats sharing a large cage. (13) One had short hair, and the other one was big and fluffy. (14) The short-haired cat raised a front paw and meowed.

(15) I said, "That's so sweet"

(16) "Those two are sisters," said the shelter manager. (17) "They need to be adopted together."

(18) That's how we got Ziggy and Pearl. (19) Ziggy chases her tail and follows me around. (20) She makes us laugh every day with her tricks. (21) Pearl can be playful, but she is much quieter. (22) She likes to curl up in a sunny window.

GO ON →

16 Which of these is a sentence fragment?

   A Sentence 2

   B Sentence 3

   C Sentence 14

   D Sentence 22

17 How can sentence 4 **best** be written?

   A Some were quiet, but they all wanted new homes.

   B Some were quiet, so they all wanted new homes.

   C Some were quiet or they all wanted new homes.

   D Some were quiet they all wanted new homes.

18 How can sentence 8 **best** be written?

   A "how would you like a cat."

   B "How would you like a cat!"

   C "How would you like a cat?"

   D "how would you like a cat?"

GO ON →

19 Which sentence is a command?

    A Sentence 6

    B Sentence 7

    C Sentence 9

    D Sentence 10

20 How should sentence 15 be written correctly?

    A I said, "That's so sweet

    B I said, "That's so sweet,"

    C I said, "That's so sweet!"

    D I said, "That's so sweet?"

Narrative Performance Task

Task:

Your class is exploring how learning helps people grow. Each student will write a story to include in a class book about learning and growing. Before your teacher assigns the story, you find two articles that give information about places where people can go to learn about the past.

After you have looked at these sources, you will answer some questions about them. Briefly scan the sources and the three questions that follow. Then, go back and read the sources carefully to gain the information you will need to answer the questions and complete your research and story.

In Part 2, you will write a story using the information you have read.

Directions for Part 1

You will now look at two sources. You can look at either of the sources as often as you like.

Research Questions:

After looking at the sources, use the rest of the time in Part 1 to answer three questions about them. Your answers to these questions will be scored. Also, your answers will help you think about the information you have read, which should help you write your story. You may refer to the sources when you think it would be helpful. You may also look at your notes.

GO ON →

Source #1: Living History

There are different ways that people can learn about history. One way is to read books. Another way is to visit towns and other places that are part of our country's past.

Williamsburg, Virginia

Williamsburg has many old buildings. They look just like they did in the 1700s. The people who work there dress like people did in the past. They tell stories about the men, women, and children who lived long ago. There are shops where people can see how things were made. There is a shop where clothing is made. There are also shops for chair makers, shoe makers, and hat makers. Visitors can sometimes try making things the way people did in the past.

Columbia, California

The town of Columbia grew into a town because gold was found nearby. People who work there dress like people did in the 1850s. Women even wear long dresses and sun hats. Most of the buildings have been there for over 160 years. Visitors can ride in a stage coach or walk through a gold mine. They can help make candles by dipping strings in wax. They can even pan for gold in creeks like people did during the gold rush.

Pueblos in the Southwest

There are many ruins of Native American pueblos. Pueblos are like apartment buildings. They are made of stone, mud, and wood. Sometimes the pueblos were built into cliffs. Many people lived in these buildings. Visitors can see how the thick mud walls kept out the desert heat. They can also see how the people grew and cooked food. Walking through the ruins gives visitors a feel of what it was like to live there.

People can read about what happened in the past in books. But visiting old places helps them understand what life was really like long ago.

GO ON →

Source #2: A Visit to the Natural History Museum

Visiting a natural history museum is a good way to learn about the past. Many cities and towns have one. The different parts of the museum can help you learn lots of things.

Dinosaur Rooms

Dinosaur rooms have the bones of animals that lived many years ago. People who study them dug up the bones from under the ground. The bones are often made into a whole skeleton. Some of the dinosaurs are huge! Pictures and scenes show the foods that they ate. Some were meat eaters, and some were plant eaters. Other scenes show ideas about how the dinosaurs died off. One museum has built big dinosaur models. They move and even make dinosaur noises.

Gem Rooms

Many museums have rooms where beautiful gems, or stones, can be seen. Some of the stones are diamonds. You can see how different stones grow inside the earth. Some stones have been cut into smaller pieces to make jewelry. One famous diamond is in a museum in Washington, D.C. It is called the Hope Diamond. This is the world's biggest dark blue diamond.

Native American Rooms

Some museums have rooms that show how Native Americans lived many years ago. People can see how they cooked, made clothing, and played games. They can see how they made tools and hunted. The museums also show different kinds of Native American houses.

Traveling Displays

King Tut was a ruler of the kingdom of Egypt many years ago. His tomb was discovered over 90 years ago. It had many wonderful things inside. Treasures of gold and jewels were found. The walls were painted with beautiful pictures. Today, a show of King Tut's treasures moves to museums in different cities. That way many people can see them.

A visit to a museum can take you back in time. It lets you have fun while you learn many wonderful things about nature and history.

GO ON →

1 Complete the chart to match each source with the sentence that states its main idea. Mark **one** box under **each** source.

	Source #1: Living History	Source #2: A Visit to the Natural History Museum
Dinosaur bones and famous gems are examples of things from history.	☐	☐
Viewing collections of things from the past is one way to learn about history.	☐	☐
Old towns in Virginia, California, and the Southwest have lots of visitors.	☐	☐
Visiting old places can help people understand history.	☐	☐

GO ON →

2 Source #1 and Source #2 tell about different ways to learn about the past. Tell **one** thing people can learn by visiting an old place and **one** thing they can learn by visiting a natural history museum. For each detail, include the source number or title.

_____

_____

_____

_____

3 Why is it important to understand the past? Use **one** example from **each** source to support your answer. For each example, include the source number or title.

_____

_____

_____

_____

_____

_____

GO ON →

Directions for Part 2

You will now look at your sources, take notes, and plan, draft, revise, and edit your story. First read your assignment and the information about how your story will be scored. Then begin your work.

Your Assignment:

Your class has decided to put together a book of stories about how people can learn about the past. Your book of stories will be read by parents, teachers, and other students in your school. Your teacher has assigned you to write a story about a trip to a natural history museum. Imagine that you and your classmates enter the museum and see many displays. Tell about what you and your classmates see and do at the museum. Tell about what you learn about the past. Your story should be several paragraphs long.

Writers usually do research to add realistic details to the setting, characters, and plot in their stories. Use information from the sources you have read to write your story. Make sure your story includes a setting, gives information about the characters, and describes what happens. Remember to use words that describe. Your story should have a clear beginning, middle, and end.

REMEMBER: A well-written story

- has a clear plot and clear sequence of events
- is well-organized and has a point of view
- uses details from the sources
- uses clear language
- follows rules of writing (spelling, punctuation, and grammar)

Now begin work on your story. Manage your time carefully so that you can plan, write, revise, and edit the final draft of your story. Write your response on a separate sheet of paper.

Read the passage. Then answer the questions.

Leaving Ireland Behind

"Wake up, Liam!" said Mum. Her voice was quiet but excited. I sat up in my bunk and looked around. The other passengers were still asleep in our dark, cramped quarters. What could Mum want? I rubbed my eyes and looked at her. She had changed into her good dress. She was holding out my best shirt and trousers. "I spoke to the Captain," Mum whispered. "Our ship will be in New York before noon."

I hopped down and took my clothes from Mum. I hurried off to change and wash up. Then Mum and I packed our things and climbed the stairs to the ship's deck. The sky was blue and cloudless. Far ahead, I could see the coast we were approaching. Our voyage from Ireland to America was finally coming to an end. Soon I would see Dad again. The thought of seeing him caused joy to fill my heart and swell up like a big balloon.

Soon other passengers joined us on the deck. Many of them had become our friends during the voyage. We all left Ireland for the same reason—life there was hard. A terrible rot had killed farmers' potatoes, our most important food. All over Ireland, people were hungry, sick, and afraid. So we left Ireland behind and hoped for a better life in America.

Dad was already there. Two years had passed since he left for New York. He was living in a tiny room in a building crowded with Irish immigrants. He worked in an iron factory. The job was hard and dangerous, and the pay was poor, but Dad did not complain. His letters home were cheerful, and each held a little money saved from his pay. When we had collected enough money, Mum bought two tickets for our voyage across the Atlantic Ocean.

I found Jack and Mary, my new friends. To pass the time, we sat on the deck and played cards. Like me, Jack and Mary were traveling with their mother to join their father in New York. Our last hours on the ship crept by. As we neared the port, passengers moved toward the front of the ship to get their first glimpse of New York.

GO ON →

Jack and Mary's mother appeared. "Go find your mum, Liam," she said. "She's looking for you." When I found Mum, she grabbed my hand and held it tightly. "Stick to me like glue now, son," she said.

The ship nosed up the East River to the port of New York. Sailors rushed about shouting instructions to one another. They lowered the anchor. Passengers who caught sight of loved ones on shore shouted, too. When the bridge was lowered, everyone crowded toward it. Mum and I picked up our bags and walked down the bridge. "Just look for the cap, Liam," Mum reminded me. She was talking about the bright red cap she'd knitted and placed on Dad's head the day he left for America.

"Wear this when you meet our ship," she said that day, "so we can find you in the crowd." With a grin, Dad answered, "I will." Now Mum and I scanned the crowd until we spotted the red cap. "Dad! Dad!" I shouted. He turned toward us and opened his arms. As we rushed to embrace him, Dad's grin seemed as wide as the ocean.

GO ON →

1 What details from the illustration **best** help you understand the passage better? Underline **two** details.

Details:

The illustration shows how crowded it is on the ship.

The illustration shows how some ships have upper decks.

The illustration shows how Liam and his mum look happy.

The illustration shows how Liam is much smaller than his mum.

The illustration shows how the ship is almost landing at a dock.

2 Read the sentence from the passage.

The thought of seeing him caused joy to fill my heart and <u>swell up like a big balloon</u>.

Which words show the mood the author creates by using the simile "swell up like a big balloon"? Pick **two** choices.

A calm

B silly

C funny

D joyful

E relaxed

F cheery

GO ON →

3   The following question has two parts. First, answer part A. Then, answer part B.

Part A: Which sentence **best** describes the main theme of the passage?

A   Learn from your mistakes.

B   It is fun to meet new people.

C   Be kind to people around you.

D   New beginnings bring new promise.

Part B: Which sentence from the passage **best** supports your answer in part A?

A   "Many of them had become our friends during the voyage."

B   "So we left Ireland behind and hoped for a better life in America."

C   "His letters home were cheerful, and each held a little money saved from his pay."

D   "Like me, Jack and Mary were traveling with their mother to join their father in New York."

GO ON →

4 The passage "Leaving Ireland Behind" tells about Liam leaving his home in Ireland. Write a brief summary of the passage, including a theme you see in the passage. Be sure to use your own words and include details from the passage.

_____

_____

_____

_____

_____

5 Read the sentence from the passage.

As we rushed to embrace him, Dad's grin seemed <u>as wide as the ocean</u>.

What does the simile "as wide as the ocean" show about the dad in the sentence?

A He is excited to travel.

B He wants to go swimming.

C He is happy to see his family.

D He wants to get on the boat.

GO ON →

Read the passage. Then answer the questions.

Bringing Back the Puffin

People call the puffin the "clown of the sea." This bird has big orange feet and a striped beak. Black and white feathers cover its short, tubby body. When it walks, it waddles like a duck. This funny-looking bird can live on land and at sea.

A Capable Animal

Puffins spend most of their lives swimming through the seas. They can drink salt water, so they do not need to come to land to get fresh water. They also dive well, plunging down 200 feet.

In the spring, older puffins gather in large groups on land. They choose mates and dig burrows, or holes, for their nests. Before long, the mother bird lays one egg. When the fuzzy chick hatches, the parents feed it lots of fish. Weeks later, the chick is big enough to leave home.

The young bird slips from its nest at night. The darkness keeps the bird unharmed as it dashes for the water. For the next few years, the puffin will live at sea. Puffins do not mate until they are about five years old.

One Scientist's Dream

The first time Stephen Kress saw puffins, he was amazed. Thousands of the birds had gathered on the shore in Canada. He knew that puffins once lived in America, too. Sadly, too much hunting had killed them.

Kress wanted to bring back puffins to America. He asked some wildlife groups to help him. After studying the birds, they figured out a plan.

A Hopeful Plan

To begin, Kress and his helpers dug burrows on an island near the state of Maine. Next, they got some chicks from Canada. They put the chicks in the burrows and fed them. The chicks grew into young birds. Soon they entered the sea.

GO ON →

Kress hoped the puffins would come back one day. Often, puffins return to their first home to mate. However, puffins also like large groups, and few birds visited Maine. To solve the problem, Kress set up wooden puffins on the island. He played recordings of the puffins' calls. He waited and waited.

A Pair Returns

Five years passed. At last, in 1981, Kress saw two puffins nesting on the island! Since that time, their number has grown. Today, over 1,000 pairs of these unusual birds nest on five of Maine's islands.

Kress and his group still help puffins. For example, in the spring, they chase away hungry gulls that might steal eggs. Thanks to their efforts, the clown of the sea lives in America again.

A puffin stands on a rock on a Maine island.

Arco/C. Wermter/©imagebroker/Alamy

GO ON →

6 The following question has two parts. First, answer part A. Then, answer part B.

Part A: Based on the information in the passage, the author would **most likely** agree with which statement?

A Scientists should stop bothering puffin families in the wild.

B It is good news that the puffins are returning to parts of America.

C Scientists need to find a way to bring back other wild animals to America.

D It would be better if puffins stayed with their parents until they are adults.

Part B: Which sentence from the passage **best** supports the answer in part A?

A "When the fuzzy chick hatches, the parents feed it lots of fish."

B "He asked some wildlife groups to help him."

C "However, puffins also like large groups, and few birds visited Maine."

D "Thanks to their efforts, the clown of the sea lives in America again."

GO ON →

7 Read the sentence from the passage.

The darkness keeps the bird <u>unharmed</u> as it dashes for the water.

What does the word <u>unharmed</u> mean?

A bothered

B careful

C safe

D shy

8 Read the paragraph from the passage.

The first time Stephen Kress saw puffins, he was amazed. Thousands of the birds had gathered on the shore in Canada. He knew that puffins once lived in America, too. Sadly, too much hunting had killed them.

What does the author show about Kress in the paragraph? Pick **two** choices.

A Kress cared about the safety of the birds when he saw them.

B Kress had never learned anything about the puffin before.

C Kress was on vacation in Canada when he saw the birds.

D Kress knew he would never see the puffin again.

E Kress was excited and interested in the puffin.

GO ON →

9 Read the sentence from the passage.

Today, over 1,000 pairs of these <u>unusual</u> birds nest on five of Maine's islands.

Complete the chart to match the word <u>unusual</u> with its meaning and with a word that uses the prefix *un-* in the same way. Mark **one** box for the meaning and **one** box for the prefix *-un*.

	The meaning of <u>unusual</u>	Uses the prefix *un-* like <u>unusual</u>
strange	☐	☐
clear	☐	☐
untrue	☐	☐
uniform	☐	☐

10 Why does the author include the information on the way the puffin looks?

  A to explain why the puffin is so scared of other animals

  B to tell why the puffin is such a special and uncommon bird

  C to compare the puffin to other birds living in the same area

  D to show why the puffin has a hard time surviving in certain climates

GO ON →

Read the poems. Then answer the questions.

There Once Was a Bird from Peru

There once was a bird from Peru,
That tipped like a plane as it flew.
In circles it went
Til all day was spent
5   Making one giant loopty-loo!

Spring Cricket

Little cricket of spring,
Sing softly in your tree.
"Come to me," you call.
"Watch me work."
5   You are happy to be alive.

Climbing up
In the sweet spring sunshine,
I whisper, "I am coming."
And I rise,
10   Ever careful and quiet.

Face to face,
We meet
And wait like statues,
And then you go about your work,
15   And I am happy, too.

GO ON →

11   Read the line from the first poem.

In circles it <u>went</u>

Which word from the poem rhymes with the word <u>went</u>?

A   was

B   like

C   flew

D   spent

12   Read the line from the first poem.

That tipped <u>like a plane</u> as it flew.

What does the simile "like a plane" show about the bird?

A   how it falls

B   how long it is

C   how it moves

D   how heavy it is

13   Read the lines from the second poem. Circle the words that start with the same sounds.

Little cricket of spring,

Sing softly in your tree.

GO ON →

Student Name _____

14 The following question has two parts. First, answer part A. Then, answer part B.

Part A: Who is the speaker in the second poem?

A someone climbing the tree

B the cricket

C the tree

D someone not in the poem

Part B: Which line from the second poem **best** supports the answer in part A?

A "Little cricket of spring,"

B "'Watch me work.'"

C "In the sweet spring sunshine,"

D "And I rise,"

15 Read the line from the second poem.

And wait like statues,

What words **best** describe the meeting between the speaker and the cricket? Pick **two** choices.

A busy

B tiring

C still

D scary

E calm

GO ON →

Read the passage below. Choose the word or words that correctly complete the sentences.

Last July, ___(1)___ had three puppies. She loved the puppies, but she knew she couldn't keep them. "Our apartment is too small for four dogs," Dad said.

"I know," said Veronica sadly.

"You can still pick the ___(2)___ names," said Mom.

Veronica felt a little better. She thought of many different names. Finally, she chose Freckles, Patch, and Snowy.

The puppies grew quickly. They were a lot to handle. The puppies ___(3)___. They scratched the doors with the claws on their ___(4)___.

When the puppies were eight weeks old, Veronica and her parents brought them to an animal shelter. A man put the puppies in a cage. Veronica felt sad again.

"Don't worry," said the man. "Several ___(5)___ come every day to look at puppies. Your puppies will have new homes very soon!"

GO ON →

16 Which answer should go in blank (1)?

    A veronica's dog

    B Veronica's dog

    C Veronica's Dog

    D Veronicas dog

17 Which answer should go in blank (2)?

    A puppies

    B puppy's

    C puppys'

    D puppies'

18 Which answer should go in blank (3)?

    A chewed on books they chewed on shoes

    B chewed on books chewed on shoes

    C chewed on books and shoes

    D chewed on books on shoes

GO ON →

19 Which answer should go in blank (4)?

    A feet

    B feets

    C foots

    D foot

20 Which answer should go in blank (5)?

    A familys

    B families

    C familyes

    D family

Informational Performance Task

Task:

Your class has been learning about different ways that problems can be solved. Now your class is going to create a magazine to share what they have learned. Each student will write an article for the magazine.

Before you decide what you will write about, you will read two articles that provide information on different ways to solve problems. After you have looked at these sources, you will answer some questions about them. Briefly scan the sources and the three questions that follow. Then, go back and read the sources carefully to gain the information you will need to answer the questions and write an informational article for the class magazine.

In Part 2, you will write your article using information from the two sources.

Directions for Part 1

You will now look at two sources. You can look at either of the sources as often as you like.

Research Questions:

After looking at the sources, use the rest of the time in Part 1 to answer three questions about them. Your answers to these questions will be scored. Also, your answers will help you think about the information you have read, which should help you write your informational article. You may refer to the sources when you think it would be helpful. You may also look at your notes.

GO ON →

Source #1: A Holiday for Trees

J. Sterling Morton thought trees were great plants. As a boy, he lived in Michigan. Tall, grand trees filled his neighborhood. Morton was amazed that some trees, like towering oaks, grew from little acorns.

A Treeless Place

In 1854, Morton and his wife moved to Nebraska. At that time, people called the prairie "the Great American Desert." Few trees grew on the grassy plain. Often, pioneers cut down the bushes they found. They used the wood for building homes or for fires. When Morton saw the empty prairie, he longed for trees.

After Morton built his cabin, he wanted to plant trees on his land. To find them, he hiked along the Missouri river. He dug up oaks, elms, and maples. He brought the trees back to his home and planted them. Slowly, his ranch grew. Next, Morton purchased fruit trees and added orchards to his fields.

Spreading the News

Morton wanted to share his love for trees with others. His work helped him find a way. Morton wrote for a newspaper, and he included stories about trees. Many people read them.

In his stories, Morton told people how trees could help them. He explained that trees gave them lumber to build things and wood for fuel. Fruit trees offered fresh food.

Trees offered other important services, too. If people planted trees near their homes, the trees would block winter winds. In the summer, the trees' thick leaves would shade their home. Last of all, the trees' roots would hold the soil near their homes in place.

Readers listened to Morton's ideas. They respected his experience. The leaders in Nebraska read Morton's stories, too. They gave him a job working for their state. He could guide their use of land.

GO ON →

A Special Day

Morton's new job allowed him to talk with the state's leaders. At one meeting, Morton put forward a plan. He wanted the state to have a holiday for planting trees. They would call it "Arbor Day." Morton chose the word *arbor* because it means "tall, woody plant."

The leaders agreed with Morton. On April 10, 1872, Nebraska celebrated the first Arbor Day. In their schools, each class planted a tree. In Nebraska City, the children held a parade. They marched through town with banners. The children went to the city opera house. Crowds filled the seats. They listened to Morton tell them about trees, and they sang songs. That day, people across the state planted about a million trees!

Around the World

Morton's new holiday was a big success. In time, all 50 states followed Nebraska's example. Today, the tree-planting day has spread to other countries, too. Morton found a way to share his love for trees with the whole world.

GO ON →

Source #2: Searching for Lost Treasure

As a young boy, Barry Clifford loved to listen to his uncle's stories. His favorite one was about a pirate ship named the *Whydah*. In 1717, the ship had sunk not far from the Cape Cod coast. At the time, it was carrying a fortune in gold.

For years, people wondered where the treasure might be. Some guessed that soon after the ship sank, eager men swam out to the wreck and grabbed the gold. However, others thought the Whydah's riches were hiding under the sea. When Clifford grew older, he set out to find the prize.

Putting Together a Plan

At first, Clifford spent his time in libraries. He read old stories and records about the ship. The stories gave him clues. Clifford found out that one sea captain had tried to recover the sunken ship. The captain failed, but he left behind his maps. Clifford studied the maps. They showed him the best places to search.

A Tiring Hunt

Clifford was excited to begin his treasure hunt. He gathered a crew of divers to help him. His team worked from a boat. They used machines like a *magnetometer*. This machine gave off a signal when it passed over a piece of metal. Guided by the signals, the men dove into the sea. They dug in the sand to find the metal things.

For two years, the divers had little luck. Often, they found junk like steel rods. Some men wanted to quit, but Clifford did not give up. At last, an amazed diver splashed to the surface. He shouted that he had spied three cannons!

GO ON →

Crusty Treasures

In a flash, the crew dove into the water. They rescued one cannon. Sea minerals covered its metal, so it looked like a big rock. The crew also gathered some crusty lumps. Clifford broke one lump apart. Inside, was a coin from 1688. Clifford had found the treasure.

A Look into History

In time, Clifford and his crew recovered thousands of items from the shipwreck. The riches included hundreds of gold and silver coins. There were gold bars, rings, and necklaces.

The crew also saved things like spoons, pens, and builders' tools. They found buttons, buckles, and dishes. These parts of the treasure had a different value. They taught people about the pirates' lives. For example, the pens showed that some of the pirates knew how to write.

Today, Clifford's treasure is worth millions of dollars. If he sold the items, he could be rich. Instead, Clifford has put the treasure in a museum. In this way, he can share his favorite story with other people.

GO ON →

Student Name _____

1   Complete the chart to match each source to a detail from the
     source. Mark **one** box next to **each** detail.

	Source #1: A Holiday for Trees	Source #2: Searching for Lost Treasure	Both Source #1 and Source #2
Reaching a goal as an adult can start from something that happened during one's childhood.	☐	☐	☐
Using a good idea can help people set an example in their own lives.	☐	☐	☐
Asking people for help is sometimes needed when solving a problem.	☐	☐	☐

GO ON →

2 Explain what would have happened if Morton and Clifford did not have a plan on how they were going to reach their goals. Give at least **two** details, one from Source #1 and one from Source #2, to support your answer. For each detail, include the source title or number.

_____

_____

_____

_____

_____

3 Explain what was learned because of Morton's and Clifford's work. Use **one** detail from **each** source to support your explanation. For each detail, include the source title or number.

_____

_____

_____

_____

_____

_____

GO ON →

Directions for Part 2

You will now look at your sources, take notes, and plan, draft, revise, and edit your article for the magazine. First read your assignment and the information about how your informational article will be scored. Then begin your work.

Your Assignment:

Your class is creating a magazine about solving problems. For your part in the magazine, you have decided to write an informational article about what it takes to solve a problem. Your article will be read by other students, teachers, and parents.

Using information from the two sources, "A Holiday for Trees" and "Searching for Lost Treasure," develop a main idea about what it takes to solve a problem. Choose the most important information from the sources to support your main idea. Then, write an informational article. It should be several paragraphs long. Clearly organize your article and support your main idea with details from the sources.

Use your own words except when quoting directly from the sources. Be sure to give the source title or number when using details from the sources.

REMEMBER: A well-written informational article

- has a clear main idea
- is well-organized and stays on topic
- has an introduction and conclusion
- uses transitions
- uses details from the sources to support the main idea
- develops ideas fully
- uses clear language
- follows rules of writing (spelling, punctuation, and grammar)

Now begin work on your informational article. Manage your time carefully so that you can plan, write, revise, and edit the final draft of your article. Write your response on a separate sheet of paper.

Read the passage. Then answer the questions.

The Wise Man

Long ago there was a wise man who lived in a village. The villagers came to the wise man with their problems. He always listened carefully and then gave help or advice. He found a way to solve every problem under the sun. In this way, the villagers came to count on the wise man.

Time went by, and the wise man grew old. The villagers began to worry. "The wise man will not live forever," they said. "Who will give us help and advice when he is gone?"

The villagers went to the wise man's house and explained their problem to him, and the wise man listened carefully. Then he said, "I know how to solve this problem."

"Tell us what to do, wise man," the villagers said.

The wise man replied, "Several clever young men live in our village. Choose the three who are the cleverest. Send them to my house this evening. I shall put them to a test. The young man who passes the test will be the next wise man of the village."

"We will do as you say," said the villagers.

After the villagers left, the wise man went outside and whistled for his friend Nightingale. The bird flew from her nest in a tree beside the wise man's house and settled at his feet. "What do you want, Wise Man?" Nightingale asked.

"Tonight when the sky is dark, fly to a tree many miles from here," the wise man replied. "When you reach the tree, sing your saddest song. As you sing, say, 'Help me! I cannot find my way home!'"

"Is that all?" asked Nightingale.

GO ON →

"Not quite," the wise man said. "If a young man comes to help you, tell him where you live. If he offers to return you to your nest, go with him."

Nightingale was agreeable to her friend's plan. "I will do as you ask," she said.

The wise man went inside and prepared a large dinner. Soon, three young men appeared at his door. The wise man invited them inside. "We shall eat and talk so I can learn a little about each of you," the wise man said.

The young men thought this was the wise man's test for them. During the dinner they did their best to make clever remarks. When the dinner was over, the wise man asked the young men to stay the night. He also invited them to breakfast the next morning and said, "Meet me at sunrise. I will tell you then who will become the next wise man."

At sunrise, only two young men joined the wise man for breakfast. "We will wait for our other friend," the wise man said.

Just then, the door to the house opened, and the third young man walked in. He looked worn out and sleepy.

"I am sorry that I am late," the young man said. "Last night, a nightingale's song woke me from my sleep. She was singing sadly because she could not find her way home. So I walked and walked until I found her. Just now I returned her to her nest beside this house."

The wise man smiled and said, "You have passed my test. You will be the next wise man."

His words puzzled the three young men. "Please explain," they said.

"All of you are clever, but a wise man must also be able to listen carefully when people explain their problems. Only then can he offer the best help and advice." The wise man added, "A man who is a servant to a nightingale's call for help is a good listener indeed."

GO ON →

1 Read the paragraph from the passage.

Time went by, and the wise man grew old. The villagers began to worry. "The wise man will not live forever," they said. "Who will give us help and advice when he is gone?"

Why is the paragraph important to the plot?

A It tells why the nightingale is needed.

B It tells why the villagers have a problem.

C It tells how the young men will be tested.

D It tells how the main problem will be solved.

2 The following question has two parts. First, answer part A. Then, answer part B.

Part A: What is the **main** problem in the passage?

A A village must find a new wise man.

B A nightingale has lost her way home.

C A man must bring a bird back to her nest.

D A group of men must impress a wise man.

Part B: Which sentence from the passage **best** supports the answer in Part A?

A "He always listened carefully and then gave help or advice."

B "'Who will give us help and advice when he is gone?'"

C "'If a young man comes to help you, tell him where you live.'"

D "During the dinner they did their best to make clever remarks."

GO ON →

3   Read the sentence from the passage.

Nightingale was <u>agreeable</u> to her friend's plan.

Which words use the suffix *-able* in the same way as <u>agreeable</u>? Pick two choices.

A cable

B table

C stable

D fixable

E enjoyable

4   Circle the word from the paragraph that has almost the same meaning as the word <u>invited</u>.

The young men thought this was the wise man's test for them. During the dinner they did their best to make clever remarks. When the dinner was over, the wise man asked the young men to stay the night. He also <u>invited</u> them to breakfast the next morning and said, "Meet me at sunrise. I will tell you then who will become the next wise man."

5   How does the wise man solve the villagers' problem?

A He pretends that he is a nightingale.

B He proves that no one can replace him.

C He tests who will answer a nightingale's call.

D He asks the villagers to choose a new wise man.

GO ON →

Read the passage. Then answer the questions.

Strange Science

Long ago, people thought living things could come from nonliving things. People saw worms in the soil after a rainstorm. They thought the worms came from water and dirt. People found rats in garbage. They thought the rats came from rotting food. These ideas may seem laughable today. Yet they made sense to people who lived long ago.

Some scientists did not believe ideas like these, so they did experiments. Francesco Redi was one of these scientists. In 1668, he tested the idea that flies come from meat. Why did people believe this? When meat was left out, worm-like creatures called maggots appeared. Soon they turned into flies. Redi did not believe the flies came from meat.

Flies Come from Flies

For his experiment, Redi used three jars. Redi put some meat in each one. He left one jar uncovered. He covered the second jar with netting. He covered the third jar tightly. Then he waited to see what would happen.

Before long, flies appeared. They laid eggs on the meat in the first jar and on the netting of the second jar, but they stayed away from the third jar. Soon Redi found lots of maggots on the meat. He found some on the netting. The covered jar had no maggots at all. In a few days, the maggots turned into flies.

Redi proved that flies do not come from meat. They come from eggs laid by other flies. When the eggs turn into maggots, the meat is their food.

More to Prove

Redi's experiment helped to change people's minds, but only a little. He convinced many people that insects and bigger animals come from animal parents. However, people still thought tiny living things, such as germs, could come from nonliving things.

GO ON →

Two hundred years passed before another scientist put this idea to rest. His name was Louis Pasteur. He wanted to prove that germs come from other germs, not from nonliving things such as food. Pasteur's job was harder than Redi's in a way. Redi could see flies landing on meat to lay their eggs. Pasteur could not observe germs with his eyes alone.

Germs Make More Germs

For his experiment, Pasteur poured soup broth into two glass bottles. Next, he boiled the broth to kill any germs that might be in it. Then he used heat to melt and shape the tops of the bottles. Pasteur made one top a straight, open tube. He turned and twisted the other one into an S shape. If tiny living germs were in the air, Pasteur thought, they could get into the bottle with the straight tube at the top. But the other bottle's curving tube would keep germs out.

Then Pasteur waited to see what would happen. In a few weeks, he noticed something. The broth in the first bottle was cloudy, but the broth in the second bottle was clear. He used a microscope to examine broth from each bottle. In the cloudy broth, he saw living germs, but there were no germs in the clear broth. Pasteur showed that germs came from other germs. The broth did not make the germs. The germs were living in the air. Some formed a small settlement in the broth. It became food for them, so they made more germs.

Pasteur's Experiment

Before   After

Straight tube →   ← germs get in

→   Cloudy broth (experimental)

Curving tube →   ← germs stay out

→   ← Clear broth

GO ON →

Learning from Redi and Pasteur

Redi and Pasteur were special. They questioned old ideas that most people believed. They demonstrated that living things can come only from living things. They also showed us how to plan and carry out experiments. In this way, we have learned much about our world.

GO ON →

Student Name _____

6 Read the sentence from the passage.

These ideas may seem <u>laughable</u> today.

Using the suffix *-able,* what does <u>laughable</u> mean?

A after laughing

B ready to laugh

C before laughing

D not able to laugh

7 Explain why the author wrote the section "More to Prove" after the section "Flies Come from Flies." Use details from the passage to support your answer.

_____

_____

_____

_____

_____

GO ON →

8 Complete the chart to show the order of events in Pasteur's experiment. Mark **one** box next to **each** event.

	First	Second	Third	Fourth
Pasteur boiled the soup broth.	☐	☐	☐	☐
Pasteur found germs in the bottle with the straight tube top.	☐	☐	☐	☐
Pasteur put soup broth into two bottles.	☐	☐	☐	☐
Pasteur used a straight and a twisted tube for the bottle tops.	☐	☐	☐	☐

9 Read the sentence from the passage.

He covered the third jar <u>tightly</u>.

What does the word <u>tightly</u> show about the jar?

A   It's broken.

B   It's clear inside.

C   It's hard to open.

D   It's filled to the top.

GO ON →

10   The following question has two parts. First, answer part A. Then, answer part B.

Part A: Which sentence **best** explains what the passage is about?

A   Redi and Pasteur were scientists who showed that life cannot come from things that are not alive.

B   Redi and Pasteur were scientists who proved that the old ideas people believed were right.

C   Most people believed that animals such as rats and flies came from garbage and soil.

D   Most people did not think it was a good idea to support the experiments on animals.

Part B: Which sentence from the passage **best** supports the answer in Part A?

A   "They thought the worms came from water and dirt."

B   "In 1668, he tested the idea that flies come from meat."

C   "When meat was left out, worm-like creatures called maggots appeared."

D   "They demonstrated that living things can come only from living things."

GO ON →

Read the passage. Then answer the questions.

How Soil is Formed

Have you ever observed a plant growing on a cracked rock? How does this happen? Look closely. You will see tiny bits of soil in the crack. Air, water, and living things can break rock into tiny pieces. These tiny pieces can eventually become soil.

Soil is a place where most plants grow. It is a habitat for many different animals. It also holds water and nutrients used by many living things. Soil is a mixture made of rock and tiny parts of once living things. It is created when rock is slowly broken down into smaller pieces, or *weathered*.

How does rock become soil? First, solid rock is broken into smaller chunks. Over time, plants begin to grow. Their roots break the rock into smaller pieces. Plants attract other living things. The plants and other living things eventually die. Then decomposers, such as fungi, bacteria, and worms, break down the once-living things. This forms a mixture called *humus*.

After the humus is created, it is mixed with air and other materials by living things. Earthworms and animals carry humus through the soil. They also break up and loosen hard sections of soil. As they move, they create spaces where water and air can enter the soil. This speeds up the weathering process.

Over time, weathering and mixing create layers of soil. If you were to dig a deep hole through the ground, you would see the differences in each layer.

GO ON →

Layers of Soil		
Layer	What It Mostly Has	Characteristics
A	Humus	Dark in color; plant roots grow; holds water easily
B	Minerals; bits of rock and clay	Light in color; water drips from layer A
C	Large pieces of weathered rock	No plant roots or living things

All soil is formed the same way, but it can have different things in it. Soil can have sand, silt, or clay particles. Sandy soil has large particles. Clay soils have the smallest particles. Some soil is good for growing plants, while other soil is not. This has a lot to do with the amount of humus, minerals, and nutrients in the soil. They make a difference in how well plants can grow.

Soil is not just part of the ground we walk on. It is important to all living things. Most plants need soil to grow. Without the right type of soil, farmers would not be able to grow crops. All of the foods we eat depend in some way on soil.

GO ON →

11 The following question has two parts. First, answer part A. Then, answer part B.

Part A: Which sentence **best** states the main idea of the passage?

A   A mixture called humus is one of the layers found in soil.

B   Soil is very important for farmers who use it to grow crops.

C   Soil is formed from many different things that together support life.

D   A rock that gets broken down into smaller rocks attracts bacteria.

Part B: Which sentence from the passage **best** supports your answer in part A?

A   "It is a habitat for many different animals."

B   "Soil is a mixture made of rock and tiny parts of once-living things."

C   "Earthworms and animals carry humus through the soil."

D   "If you were to dig a deep hole through the ground, you would see the differences in each layer."

GO ON →

12 Circle **two** words from the paragraph that have almost the same meaning as the word <u>observed</u>.

Have you ever <u>observed</u> a plant growing on a cracked rock? How does this happen? Look closely. You will see tiny bits of soil in the crack. Air, water, and living things can break rock into tiny pieces. These tiny pieces can eventually become soil.

13 What words are **most** helpful to understanding what the chart is about?

A "layers of soil"

B "what it mostly has"

C "water drips"

D "weathered rock"

14 Look at the chart. Why might Layer A be good for growing plants? Pick **two** choices.

A It doesn't have any living things.

B The soil has a healthy color.

C There are no plant roots.

D It holds water easily.

E It has pieces of rock.

GO ON →

15 Read the sentence from the passage.

Sandy soil has large particles.

What does the word sandy mean?

A look like sand

B be without sand

C have sand

D be in need of sand

GO ON →

The draft below needs revision. Read the draft. Then answer the questions.

My Uncle Dan

(1) My Uncle Dan is a nature writer. (2) He explores wild places. (3) He writes a book about each place. (4) One of his books won a prize. (5) Uncle Dan felt very proud.

(6) Every summer I take a trip with Uncle Dan. (7) I enjoy our trips together. (8) Last summer we traveled to Arches National Park in Utah. (9) There is no place like it in the world! (10) It is filled with all kinds of life. (11) There were lizards, squirrels, and eagles. (12) Wildflowers bloomed beside the paths. (13) Uncle Dan took a picture of me on a huge rock. (14) My picture will be in his next book.

GO ON →

16 Which sentence contains a present-tense verb?

    A Sentence 3

    B Sentence 4

    C Sentence 8

    D Sentence 14

17 What is the **best** way to combine sentences 2 and 3?

    A He writes a book, he explores wild places.

    B He explores wild places, writes a book about each place.

    C He explores wild places and writes a book about each place.

    D He writes about each wild place, and he explores each place.

18 Which sentence contains a past-tense verb?

    A Sentence 3

    B Sentence 5

    C Sentence 7

    D Sentence 9

GO ON →

19   How can sentence 11 **best** be written with an action verb?

   A   Lizards, squirrels, and eagles were there.

   B   Seen were lizards, squirrels, and eagles.

   C   We saw lizards, squirrels, and eagles.

   D   Lizards were there, and squirrels and eagles.

20   Which sentence contains a future-tense verb?

   A   Sentence 11

   B   Sentence 12

   C   Sentence 13

   D   Sentence 14

Opinion Performance Task

Task:

Your class has learned about how different animals can be from each other and how people study them. Now your class is creating a website about the most interesting and unique, or different, animals. You have been asked to write an article for the website about the most unique animal. Before you decide what you will write, you read two sources that provide information about unique animals and how people try to observe and study them.

After you have looked at these sources, you will answer some questions about them. Briefly scan the sources and the three questions that follow. Then, go back and read the sources carefully to gain the information you will need to answer the questions and write an opinion article for your class website.

In Part 2, you will write your article using information from the two sources.

Directions for Part 1

You will now look at two sources. You can look at either of the sources as often as you like.

Research Questions:

After looking at the sources, use the rest of the time in Part 1 to answer three questions about them. Your answers to these questions will be scored. Also, your answers will help you think about the information you have read, which should help you write your article. You may refer to the sources when you think it would be helpful. You may also look at your notes.

GO ON →

Source #1: A Big Underwater Mystery

Long ago, sailors told stories about a sea monster in the deep ocean. It had huge arms that looked like snakes. If ships disappeared, sailors blamed the sea monster.

As years passed, some of these strange sea monsters washed up on ocean shores. After spending their lives deep in the ocean, their large bodies eventually drifted to land. Curious scientists began studying the bodies. They realized the "sea monsters" were giant squid.

A Hidden Home

The giant squid does not attack boats, but it does live in the deep sea. It swims far below the surface where little light reaches. Its cold, dark home hides the squid well. This is why it is difficult to learn its secrets.

Understanding Body Clues

However, studying the squid's body did give scientists some clues. For example, the squid has big eyes. They are the size of dinner plates. With such eyes, the squid can see well in the dark. It can skillfully hunt for fish.

The scientists also looked at the squid's head, called a mantle. It has strong muscles. That means the squid can swim fast. The mantle also has fins to help the squid through the water. Last of all, the mantle has a sharp beak, or mouth. In a flash, the squid can bite a fish into small pieces.

The squid's arms offered hints about its life, too. It has eight arms and two feeding arms, or tentacles. The tentacles are very long. They can shoot out like a net. With them, a sneaky squid can catch a fish that is 30 feet away.

GO ON →

Spying on the Squid

Scientists wanted to know more about the interesting creature. One man, Clyde Roper, tried a new trick. He placed some special cameras on some sperm whales. The whales live in the same deep waters as the squid. Roper hoped the cameras might record a squid. Instead, the movies just showed how whales feed.

Next, Roper put a camera on a small machine. From a boat, he guided the machine with a computer. The machine dove down 2,400 feet. However, it did not find a squid.

Success at Last

A woman named Edith Widder had another idea. She thought about the squid's big eyes. Perhaps the camera's bright lights frightened the squid away. To fix that problem, she made a camera that used a dim red light.

Widder and some other scientists tried her new camera. They lowered the machine deep into the sea. On their second try, they watched a squid swim toward the camera. Its legs opened wide and grabbed the machine. Since that time, other cameras have also recorded the squid.

Scientists are excited. Viewing the squid in its own home offers the best information. For instance, they saw one squid's skin change colors. By using their machines, scientists hope they will discover many more of the squid's mysterious secrets.

GO ON →

Source #2: An Uncommon Treasure

A thousand years ago, people in China sent the leader of Japan a gift. The unusual present was two giant panda bears. The animals only lived in China at the time, so few people had ever seen them.

Americans did not meet their first panda until 1936. A woman, Ruth Harkness, visited China. Some explorers helped her find a cub. She brought the bear to a zoo in America. People fell in love with the black and white bear.

A Snowy, Cold Home

Pandas make their home in the mountains of China. Bamboo trees grow on the hills. In the winter, snow covers the ground. Pandas like to wander through the thick, cold forests. Usually, they live alone.

An Animal in Danger

Over the years, some people hunted pandas. The people sold their furs for money. Slowly, the number of pandas dropped. At last, China passed laws to stop hunters. However, few pandas were left.

A Peek at Panda Life

People wanted to be sure that pandas survived. Because of this, certain zoos started to raise pandas. Today, about 300 pandas live in zoos.

The zoo pandas give scientists a chance to closely study the bears. One zoo did tests to see what kind of bamboo pandas like best. Bamboo is a plant that is the panda's main food. They have an extra thumb that helps them hold the branches as they eat.

The pandas munched their zoo lunch for about 16 hours a day. Their favorite choice was arrow bamboo. The scientists hope the information they learn from zoo pandas can help wild pandas.

GO ON →

Protected Places

In China, reserves provide a safe home for pandas. Reserves are large areas of land set aside for animals. In the reserves, the scientists take care of pandas that need help. For example, they raise cubs without mothers.

Scientists also study the reserve's pandas. For one project, scientists looked at how far pandas travel to eat. To do this, the scientists put special collars on certain bears. The collars gave off signals, so the scientists could see where the bears went.

The scientists learned that pandas often ate their food in one small area. Horses in the reserves ate bamboo in that place, too. Scientists realized the bears might not have enough food.

Into the Wild

One man, George Schaller, wanted to study pandas in their mountain home. For several years, he tracked pandas in the forests. He measured how much bamboo they ate. In two years, he only saw a panda 16 times. The shy creatures hid well.

Schaller discovered one sad problem. People continued to hunt pandas. Because of his findings, China put more force into laws guarding the bears.

Today, about 1600 pandas live in the mountains of China. Scientists continue to study them in different ways. They hope their new knowledge will help the number of pandas grow.

GO ON →

Student Name _____

1   Complete the chart to match each idea on top of the chart with
     its supporting detail. Mark **one** box under **each** idea.

	Animals' bodies help them in different ways.	Some animals can be very hard to find.
Squid have no way to see in the dark.	☐	☐
Pandas have an extra thumb that helps them hold bamboo.	☐	☐
Pandas live with other animals in the mountains.	☐	☐
Squid live in deep, dark places.	☐	☐

GO ON →

2 Source #1 discusses ways that people have tried to learn more about squid. Explain how the information in Source #2 adds to the reader's understanding of how people can learn about different animals. Give **two** details from Source #2 to support your explanation.

_____

_____

_____

_____

3 Explain why people want to observe animals in the wild. Why would this be helpful? Give **two** examples, one from Source #1 and one from Source #2. For each reason, include the source title or number.

_____

_____

_____

_____

_____

GO ON →

Directions for Part 2

You will now look at your sources, take notes, and plan, draft, revise, and edit your article. First, read your assignment and the information about how your article will be scored. Then begin your work.

Your Assignment:

Your class is creating a website about interesting animals. You have been asked to write an article about an animal that is special in some way. The article will be posted on the class website for students, parents, and teachers to read.

Your assignment is to use the information from the sources to write an article. The article should explain how one of the animals you learned about is special and different from other animals. You should also explain why the animal you chose is especially interesting. Make sure you clearly state your opinion and write several paragraphs supporting your opinion with reasons and details from the sources. Develop your ideas clearly and use your own words, except when quoting directly from the sources. Be sure to give the source title or number for the details or facts you use.

REMEMBER: A well-written opinion article

- has a clear opinion
- is well-organized and stays on topic
- has an introduction and conclusion
- uses transitions
- uses details or facts from the sources to support the opinion
- puts the information from the sources in quotes when necessary
- gives the title or number of the source for the details or facts included
- develops ideas clearly
- uses clear language
- follows rules of writing (spelling, punctuation, and grammar)

Now begin work on your opinion article. Manage your time carefully so that you can plan, write, revise, and edit the final draft of your opinion article. Write your response on a separate sheet of paper.

Read the passage. Then answer the questions.

School Play

Carmen had always dreamed of being on stage. She was thrilled when she got her first big break with a part in the school play. The teacher told her she could play the part of the doctor. She would wear a long, white doctor's coat with a stethoscope around her neck. She would also carry a big bag that held a newspaper with blank pages and a box of bandages. Carmen would say some lines. She would act funny and try to make her friends laugh. She could hardly wait to act in a real play on stage and see her dream come true.

As the day of the play approached, Carmen began to worry about being on stage. She just could not learn her lines well enough to remember her part. She sat in her bedroom, saying the lines over and over again. They just would not stick in her head. She practiced for several days and still could not remember her lines. It would be terrible if she forgot her lines on stage. She thought for a long time and decided to quit the play. She still wanted to be in the play very much, but she did not want to risk making a fool of herself in front of an audience.

Carmen went downstairs to tell the news to her family. She walked into the kitchen and announced that she would not be in the play.

"Don't worry so much," Carmen's father said, hugging her. "You're a talented young girl. You are a natural performer."

"Yes," her mother agreed. "You'll do better if you relax."

Carmen knew they were right, but she could not stop worrying. The thought of going on stage made her a bundle of nerves. The school play was the next day, and she still could not remember her part no matter how much she practiced her lines.

GO ON →

When Carmen's mother said it was bedtime, she still did not know her lines. But when she woke up the next morning, Carmen had a great idea. She took the newspaper out of the bag and opened it up. Then she wrote all her lines on the blank page. Now she could look at the newspaper and no one would know that she was reading her lines. This would help her relax and remain calm.

That day, Carmen went on stage. She said her first line. Then she said her next line. Carmen did not have to look at the newspaper once. Remembering her lines was easy because she was calm and relaxed. As a result, Carmen remembered everything. When the play was over, Carmen's parents applauded the loudest. After the play, they went backstage. Carmen's parents rushed over to congratulate her on a job well done.

"You were great!" her mother said as she hugged Carmen and smiled.

"I told you you're a star," her father said proudly.

GO ON →

1   The following question has two parts. First, answer part A. Then, answer part B.

Part A: Which detail shows how Carmen's parents felt about her performance?

A   They waited until everyone left to go backstage.

B   They sat in the back row of the auditorium.

C   They clapped more than anyone else.

D   They showed up late to the play.

Part B: Which sentence from the passage **best** supports the answer in part A?

A   "'Don't worry so much,' Carmen's father said, hugging her."

B   "But when she woke up the next morning, Carmen had a great idea."

C   "When the play was over, Carmen's parents applauded the loudest."

D   "After the play, they went backstage."

2   Read the sentence from the passage.

The thought of going on stage made her a bundle of nerves.

What does "a bundle of nerves" show about Carmen?

A   She is carrying lots of things.

B   She feels scared about performing.

C   She needs help with her costumes.

D   She thinks the stage doesn't look good.

GO ON →

3   What lesson does Carmen learn in the passage? Use details from the passage to support your answer.

_____

_____

_____

_____

4   Read the paragraph below. Circle the word that helps you figure out the meaning of the word <u>announced</u>.

Carmen went downstairs to tell the news to her family. She walked into the kitchen and <u>announced</u> that she would not be in the play.

5   What does the picture do to help the reader understand the passage? Pick **two** choices.

   A   The picture shows that people enjoy the play.

   B   The picture shows what Carmen did to prepare.

   C   The picture shows how Carmen uses the newspaper.

   D   The picture shows why Carmen is nervous about the play.

   E   The picture shows that Carmen becomes calm and has fun.

   F   The picture shows that there are not many people at the play.

GO ON →

Read the passage. Then answer the questions.

Humpback Whales

Santa Cruz, California, was buzzing with excitement in November of 2011. A pod of humpback whales was feeding so close to shore that people could see them from the beaches. Humpbacks are fun to watch. These 40-ton whales can leap completely out of the water. Then they smack into the water on their backs.

A surfer and two kayakers went out to get a closer look. Suddenly, two giant whales burst out of the water only a few feet away. The people were shocked but unhurt. The scene was captured in a photo that appeared in many magazines and on the Internet.

Whales on the Move

Why were the whales so close to shore? Humpbacks eat small fish called anchovies, among other things. In the fall of 2011, weather conditions forced big schools of anchovies toward the coast. The whales were just following their food.

These whales were migrating from north to south. Humpbacks spend the summer months in cooler waters near the poles. Then every fall they swim to warmer waters near the equator. These particular whales move to warm waters off the coast of Mexico. There they raise their babies, or calves. All winter, mothers and calves relax in the warm water. The immature whales stay close to their mothers.

Humpbacks have one of the longest migrations of any animal. It's a long trip. By migrating, the whales are adapting to the annual change of seasons. Following fish in to shore is another way they adapt.

Mammals of the Sea

Unlike most other sea creatures, whales are mammals. Mammals, such as humans, cows, and elephants, feed their babies milk. Whales are different from most mammals because they live in the ocean.

GO ON →

Whales have a thick layer of fat called blubber. It keeps them warm in cold ocean waters. It also gives them energy when they can't find food.

Whales are strong swimmers. Their smooth-skinned bodies zoom through the water. Unlike other mammals, whales have no real hair or fur, which would slow them down. Not even their ears or noses stick out. These are tucked into tiny openings in their skin.

Like all mammals, whales breathe air. They must surface to breathe. But they are not able to spend all their time on the surface. That's why their lungs are huge. Whales breathe out in a big spout that looks like steam. Then they breathe in deeply and dive. Some whales can hold their breath for an hour.

Humpback whales are known for their songs. They make sounds like moans and cries. These sounds happen in sequences and may last for hours. They also travel great distances through the ocean. Scientists are not sure what these songs mean, but the whales seem to communicate with one another. They may sing to attract mates.

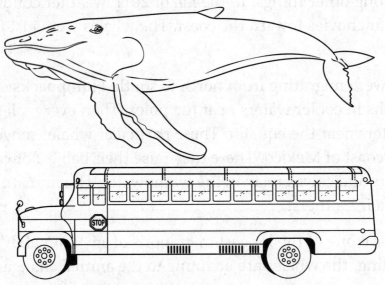

An adult humpback whale is 50 to 60 feet long.

GO ON →

6 Read the sentence from the passage.

Suddenly, two giant whales <u>burst</u> out of the water only a few feet away.

What does the word <u>burst</u> mean? Pick **two** choices.

A break out strongly

B jump up suddenly

C swim away quickly

D hide slowly

E clap loudly

7 Complete the chart to compare and contrast the features of the animals. Mark **one** box next to **each** feature.

	Whales	Other Mammals	Both
feed their babies milk	☐	☐	☐
live in the ocean	☐	☐	☐
have hair or fur	☐	☐	☐

8 The following question has two parts. First, answer part A. Then, answer part B.

Part A: What is one **difference** between whales and humans?

A Whales have lungs.

B Whales raise their babies.

C Whales communicate with each other.

D Whales hold their breath for a long time.

GO ON →

Part B: Which sentence from the passage **best** supports the answer in part A?

A "All winter, mothers and calves relax in the warm water."

B "Not even their ears or noses stick out."

C "Some whales can hold their breath for an hour."

D "Humpback whales are known for their songs."

9 What does the caption help you understand about humpback whales?

A the places whales go

B the size of the whales

C the noise whales make

D the weight of the whales

10 Read the sentence from the passage.

The <u>immature</u> whales stay close to their mothers.

The word *mature* means "developed." What does <u>immature</u> mean?

A not developed

B fully developed

C quickly developed

D almost developed

GO ON →

Read the poem. Then answer the questions.

My Dad

Here is a thing that I think is cool:
My dad teaches children here at our school.
He does more than just teach us numbers and writing,
He tries to help kids think of school as exciting.

5   He's a knight in white armor for those having trouble.
For kids who need help, he'll work more than double.
One girl in the school was failing her classes.
Dad knew she was smart and as sweet as molasses.

So he got her eyes checked, mostly to see
10   If she could distinguish between "i" and "t."
Turns out she needs glasses, and don't you suppose,
She now wears them proudly, perched on her nose.

One day a boy mentioned that he was upset
Previewing an e-mail from someone he met.
15   The boy was invited to a birthday party,
But his pockets were empty, and gifts are not free.

So Dad helped him make his own present and card,
And the boy found that making new friends is not hard.
For students who meet him, I really feel glad,
20   But much more than that, I'm just glad he's my dad.

GO ON →

11   Read the line from the poem.

Here is a thing that I think is cool:

What does the speaker think is "cool" about the dad in the poem?

A   He does a good job grading tests and projects.

B   He cares about his students and wants them to succeed.

C   He helps the other teachers if they have too much work.

D   He throws a birthday party for every student in his class.

12   The following question has two parts. First, answer part A. Then, answer part B.

Part A: What is the lesson of the poem?

A   Money is not important.

B   It is not easy to meet other people.

C   Helping others is a great thing to do.

D   All kids should have their eyes checked.

Part B: Which line from the poem **best** supports the answer in part A?

A   "For kids who need help, he'll work more than double."

B   "Turns out she needs glasses, and don't you suppose,"

C   "Previewing an e-mail from someone he met."

D   "But his pockets were empty, and gifts are not free."

GO ON →

13 Read the line from the poem.

He's a <u>knight in white armor</u> for those having trouble.

What does the poet show about the dad with the use of "knight in white armor"? Pick **two** choices.

A He wears a white suit.

B He goes into battle as a knight.

C He seems like a hero to people he helps.

D He has an unusual clothing style at school.

E He helps students who are having problems.

14 Underline the line from the poem that **best** shows how the speaker feels about his or her dad.

"One girl in the school was failing her classes."

"She now wears them proudly, perched on her nose."

"The boy was invited to a birthday party,"

"And the boy found that making new friends is not hard."

"But much more than that, I'm just glad he's my dad."

GO ON →

15 Read the lines from the poem.

So he got her eyes checked, mostly to see
If she could <u>distinguish</u> between "i" and "t."

Which of the following **best** defines <u>distinguish</u> as it is used in the poem?

A to see something clearly

B to see someone as special

C to see something as the same

D to see someone as standing out

GO ON →

Read the passage below. Choose the word or words that correctly complete the sentences.

Ray Charles was a great musician. He was born in Georgia and didn't have a lot of money growing up. He started losing his sight as a boy. By age seven, he ___(1)___ completely blind. He still had to do chores, though, such as chopping wood. Charles' mother wanted him to learn to do things for himself.

A local store owner ___(2)___ a piano, and he often let young Charles play along with him. Later, Charles went to the St. Augustine School for the Deaf and Blind in Florida where he studied music. By the time Charles was 12, people ___(3)___ him a musical genius.

By age 15, Charles had lost both parents. He couldn't pay for school, so he left Florida and moved to Seattle. There his career took off. He had many hit songs, played on TV, wrote music for movies, and ___(4)___ 18 Grammy Awards.

The song many people remember him for ___(5)___ "Georgia." He put his whole heart and soul into it. If you hear it, you won't forget it. In 1960, the state of Georgia made his recording the state song.

GO ON →

16 Which answer should go in blank (1)?

    A is

    B are

    C being

    D was

17 Which answer should go in blank (2)?

    A had

    B haved

    C have

    D has

18 Which answer should go in blank (3)?

    A calling

    B are calling

    C were calling

    D will be calling

GO ON →

19   Which answer should go in blank (4)?

    A won

    B win

    C wined

    D woned

20   Which answer should go in blank (5)?

    A will be

    B is

    C were

    D are

STOP

Narrative Performance Task

Task:

Your class has been learning about different ways to meet challenges, such as how to make friends at a new school. Now your class is going to create a class storybook to share what they have learned. Each student will write a story for the class book.

Before you decide what you will write about, you will read two articles that provide information on different ways that certain animals meet challenges. After you have looked at these sources, you will answer some questions about them. Briefly scan the sources and the three questions that follow. Then, go back and read the sources carefully to gain the information you will need to answer the questions and write a story for the class storybook.

In Part 2, you will write your story using information from the two sources.

Directions for Part 1

You will now look at two sources. You can look at either of the sources as often as you like.

Research Questions:

After looking at the sources, use the rest of the time in Part 1 to answer three questions about them. Your answers to these questions will be scored. Also, your answers will help you think about the information you have read, which should help you write your story. You may refer to the sources when you think it would be helpful. You may also look at your notes.

GO ON →

Source #1: Desert Heroes

The sun is just setting as the line of riders tops a sand dune in one of the hottest regions of the world. Long, golden rays stretch over the smooth, sandy hills. The riders climb off their camels. Then they set up camp. When the sun goes down, the desert will be very cold. The humans will huddle around campfires. But the camels will not be bothered by the chilly air. These amazing animals can handle just about anything the Sahara Desert can offer.

Ready to Roam

From head to toe, camels almost seem built for the desert. Their ears are covered with hair. This keeps out swirling sand.

The camel's eyes have two eyelids both with thick rows of long eyelashes. Bushy eyebrows rise above. Each eye also has a third eyelid. It is so thin that camels can see through it when it is closed. These eyelids protect their eyes during sandstorms that whip through the desert.

The camel has nostrils that can be closed tightly. When sand is blowing, the camel can keep from breathing it. Below those, the camel has thick lips. They help the camel eat tough desert plants.

Ship of the Desert

Many people recognize the camel because of the hump on its back. Camels in the Sahara are Arabian camels. On them, only one hump can be seen. Inside this hump, the camel can store up to 80 pounds of fat. When the camel travels across the desert, the fat is broken down into water. Because of this, camels can travel up to 100 desert miles at a time. They do not need to drink for days. This is why many people call the camel the "ship of the desert." But when camels do find water, they soak it up like a sponge. A camel can drink 30 gallons of water at one time.

GO ON →

Humans must keep their body temperature at about 98 degrees. If it is not, our bodies will work hard to make it so. But a camel will not start sweating until its body reaches more than 107 degrees. Its body will not try to warm up until it gets down to about 92 degrees inside. On cold nights, the camel's body will store the coolness. This helps keep it cooler the next day.

Fur and Patches

The outside of a camel's body is just as helpful as the inside. It is covered with thick fur. This helps the camel stay cool during the day and warm at night. The camel also has tough patches on its knees. They protect it when it kneels on hot sand.

When the camel walks, its feet spread out like snowshoes. This keeps them from sinking into the sand. Thick pads on the bottoms keep them from burning.

The ways camels have adapted are amazing. From head to toe, they are special animals. It is no wonder that humans depend on them to cross the dry Sahara Desert.

GO ON →

Source #2: The Big-Eared Fox

Far away, in the Sahara Desert in northern Africa, the sun beats down with a fierce heat. In fact, it is so hot that the sand feels like fire. Only an inch or two of rain may fall in a whole year. It does not seem that any animal could live in this place. But one of the cutest animals in the world, the fennec fox, lives there quite happily. In fact, the things that make this fox so charming are what help it to survive.

Staying Cool

The fennec fox is the smallest of all foxes. When it is full-grown, it only weighs 2–3 pounds. It measures about two feet from head to tail. But its giant ears seem like they belong to another animal. Each ear is six inches long. They point up like a bat's ears. The huge ears help the fox hear bugs, or food, that are moving under the ground. But they are not just for hearing.

In a place where temperatures can reach more than 130 degrees, cooling off is very important. When people get hot, they sweat. The sweat lets heat out of the body. However, sweat also takes water from the body. Because there is not a lot of water in the desert, fennec foxes cannot afford to lose water by sweating. Instead, their huge ears send heat out of their bodies. If you were to put your hand in front of this fox's ear, you might feel heat coming out.

Cozy Fur

While the desert is hot during the day, it can become very cold at night. The fennec fox has thick, soft fur. This cozy coat helps to keep the fox warm when it is looking for food. During the day, it protects the fox from the sun. The fur's color is creamy white. It blends with the sandy desert. This way, the fox can hide from enemies.

GO ON →

So what else about this fox protects it from the desert? The bottoms of its feet are covered with soft hair. The fox can walk safely on the hot, loose sand. Because of their shape, the feet also make good shovels. Fennec foxes sleep during the day in dens that they have dug under the ground.

Eating and Drinking

There is little food to be found in the desert. So fennec foxes eat what they find. They may eat insects, lizards, or snails. Or they may try birds, eggs, or mice. If they find any fruits or berries, they will eat those too. These desert animals can go for a long time without drinking water.

New Dangers

The charming parts of the fennec fox help it stay alive. But they also cause it danger. Sadly, many people hunt fennec foxes to sell as pets. Because of this, fewer can be seen in many parts of the desert. These foxes should be protected. This way, they can continue to enjoy life among the desert sands.

tzooka/iStock/Getty Images Plus/Getty Images

GO ON →

1 Complete the chart to match the sources to details from the sources. Mark **one** box next to **each** detail.

	Source #1: Desert Heroes	Source #2: The Big-Eared Fox	Both Source #1 and Source #2
Some desert animals can go days without drinking water.	☐	☐	☐
Some desert animals can cool down in ways besides sweating.	☐	☐	☐
Some desert animals can stay protected during sandstorms.	☐	☐	☐

GO ON →

Student Name _____

2 The sources explain how the camel and the fennec fox handle hot days and cold nights in the desert. Explain why this information is important. Use **one** example from **each** source to support your answer. For each example, include the source title or number.

_____

_____

_____

_____

3 Explain what the sources say about how the feet of the camel and fennec fox help them live in the desert. Use **one** detail from **each** source to support your explanation. For each detail, include the source title or number.

_____

_____

_____

_____

_____

GO ON →

Directions for Part 2

You will now look at your sources, take notes, and plan, draft, revise, and edit your story for the storybook. First read your assignment and the information about how your story will be scored. Then begin your work.

Your Assignment:

Your class is creating a storybook about different ways to meet challenges. Your story will be read by other students, teachers and parents. For your part in the storybook, you have decided to write a story about a family that rides a group of camels across the desert. Write about the challenges that the family faces while taking their desert adventure.

Writers often do research to add realistic details to the setting, characters, and plot in their stories. You may use information from the sources you have read to write your story. Make sure your story includes a setting, gives information about the characters, and describes what happens. Remember to use words that describe and don't just tell. Your story should have a clear beginning, middle, and end.

REMEMBER: A well-written story

- has a clear plot and clear sequence of events
- is well-organized and has a point of view
- uses details from the sources to support the story
- uses clear language
- follows rules of writing (spelling, punctuation, and grammar)

Now begin work on your story. Manage your time carefully so that you can plan, write, revise, and edit the final draft of your story. Write your response on a separate sheet of paper.

Copyright © McGraw-Hill Education

Read the passage. Then answer the questions.

Three Billy Goats

Once upon a time, there were three billy goat brothers named Biff, Bill, and Bo. Biff was the oldest brother, Bill was the middle brother, and Bo was the youngest. The billy goats were always starving. All day long they shuffled from meadow to meadow, searching for green grass under the sun's hot rays. One day, the brothers saw a stream, and on the other side of the stream was a big meadow.

"The meadow could satisfy us for the whole day," said Bill. So they trotted off toward the stream.

"Oh, dear!" Bo exclaimed when he saw it up close. "The water appears to be too deep and swift for wading, and none of us can swim."

"But look, this stream has a bridge," Biff pointed out, "so we can simply walk across it."

"No, we can't!" exclaimed Bill. "An awful troll lives under the bridge, and I'm terrified of him!"

"If we try to cross the bridge, the troll will have us for lunch!" cried Bo.

"I disagree," Biff answered calmly. "The troll is mean, but he is foolish as well, and I have a plan to outsmart him. If we stick together and follow my plan, we will surely get across the bridge."

Bill and Bo drew close and listened to Biff's idea. They agreed it was a crafty plan that could possibly work. They could hardly wait to put it into action. The three brothers trotted off to the bridge and lined up to cross it.

Bo was first, Bill was next, and Biff was last. Bo started across the bridge, trotting along and declaring loudly, "Here I come over the bridge!" In a flash, the troll hopped up from beneath the bridge and stood in his way.

GO ON →

"You won't cross the bridge," snarled the mean old troll, "because I am going to eat you!"

"Oh," said Bo, "I'm such a tiny billy goat, but my big brother Bill is right behind me. Why don't you eat him instead?"

The troll thought for a moment and said, "You're right, little goat. I should save my appetite for your big brother." So the troll stepped aside, and Bo crossed the bridge.

Next, Bill started across the bridge, trotting along and declaring loudly, "Here I come over the bridge!" The troll stood in the middle of the bridge to block Bill's way.

"You won't cross the bridge," growled the mean old troll, "because I am going to eat you!"

"Oh!" said Bill, "I'm a rather small billy goat, but my big brother Biff is right behind me. Why don't you eat him instead?"

"Well," replied the troll, "you would be a good meal for me, but your big brother would be even better!" So the troll stepped aside, and Bill crossed the bridge.

At last, it was Biff's turn to cross the bridge, but he did not trot along. Instead he put his head down and ran straight for the mean old troll. Biff smacked into the troll and pushed him off the bridge! The troll tumbled into the stream, and as the swift water carried the troll away, Biff trotted merrily across the bridge to join his brothers.

"It's just like you told us, Biff," said Bo. "We stuck together and followed our plan, and now we have another meadow of grass to eat."

GO ON →

1 The following question has two parts. First, answer part A. Then, answer part B.

Part A: Based on the passage, how do Bill and Bo view their brother?

A They think he is clever.

B They think he is selfish.

C They think he is foolish.

D They think he is funny.

Part B: Which sentence from the passage **best** supports the answer in Part A?

A "All day long they shuffled from meadow to meadow, searching for green grass under the sun's hot rays."

B "'If we try to cross the bridge, the troll will have us for lunch!' cried Bo."

C "They agreed it was a crafty plan that could possibly work."

D "In a flash, the troll hopped up from beneath the bridge and stood in his way."

GO ON →

2 What do the troll and the goats think about each other? Circle the **best** option for **each** blank.

The three billy goats think that the troll is _____ while the troll thinks the goats are _____ to try to cross the bridge.

<u>Options for Blank 1</u>

honest

unkind

caring

<u>Options for Blank 2</u>

silly

brave

helpful

3 Read the sentences from the passage.

"I <u>disagree</u>," Biff answered calmly. "The troll is mean, but he is foolish as well, and I have a plan to outsmart him."

If the word *agree* means "to give one's approval," what does <u>disagree</u> mean? Pick **two** choices.

A to be alike

B to get along well

C to oppose an idea

D to understand each other

E to have a different opinion

GO ON →

Student Name _____

4 What do the brothers think about Biff's idea to cross the stream at the beginning of the passage and at the end? Use details from the passage to support your answer.

_____

_____

_____

_____

_____

5 Read the sentence from the passage.

Bo started across the bridge, trotting along and declaring loudly, "Here I come over the bridge!"

Which word is a homophone for the word here?

A home

B hear

C hair

D hurry

GO ON →

Copyright © McGraw-Hill Education

Read the passage. Then answer the questions.

Marconi's Great Invention

In the late 1800s, important news traveled by telegraph. Messages were sent across wires in Morse code, a set of short and long clicks or dots and dashes that stand for letters of the alphabet. Messages could be sent anywhere that had telegraph lines, but there was a problem with the system. People could not send messages without wires.

During this time, there was a young man in Italy named Guglielmo Marconi who was very interested in electricity and radio waves. Marconi knew that radio waves carry electric signals through the air. So, in 1895, he worked on sending wireless signals from one distance to another. He tried using different metal shapes. He wanted to see what would work best. Every test he ran taught him something. Soon he was sending wireless signals a mile away.

Marconi thought his invention could be used to send messages. But no scientists in Italy were interested. So, in 1896 he went to England. There, he got help from the post office. Later in that year he received a patent for his wireless telegraphy. This meant that for a period of time he had the right to be the only one who could make or sell his product. He began showing his invention to the public.

In 1897, Marconi started his own wireless telegraph company. In the same year he showed the telegraph to the Italian government. He was able to send a wireless signal twelve miles away. He began sending wireless signals farther and farther. In 1899 he sent a wireless signal across the English Channel. This is the body of water between England and France. Then he set up his machines on two American ships. They sent news about a boat race to New York newspapers. Marconi became world famous.

GO ON →

Marconi did not stop there. He kept making his invention better. Most scientists believed radio waves could not travel far. They thought the waves would shoot into space instead of hugging the curves of Earth. Marconi wanted to prove them wrong. In 1901, he sent wireless signals across the Atlantic Ocean. The signals were sent from England to Canada. The signals traveled a distance of about 2,100 miles.

In 1909 Marconi won the Nobel Prize for his work. He patented several new inventions between the years of 1902 and 1912. His company made lots of money. Marconi was now rich and famous. But he never stopped tinkering. He and others worked to make his invention even better. Some scientists used it to carry voices and music. In 1920, the first public radio station went on the air. Radios were the messengers that brought news and music into homes across the world.

Today, more things than ever are wireless. Radio, TV, and cell phones use radio waves. Marconi's ideas and hard work made all this happen. When he died in 1937, radio stations around the world agreed to be silent for two minutes. They did this to honor Marconi's successes.

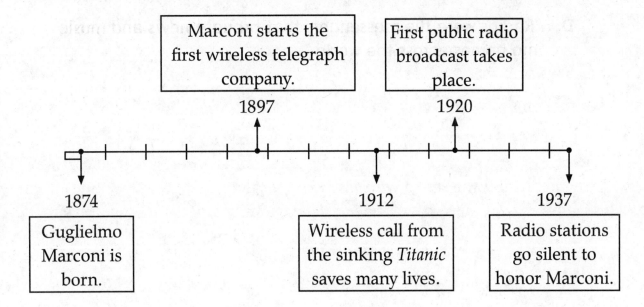

GO ON →

6 The following question has two parts. First, answer part A. Then, answer part B.

Part A: Why couldn't people send messages across the Atlantic Ocean before Marconi's invention?

A   Morse code was not invented yet.

B   People could not travel that far at that time.

C   Messages could only be sent places through wires.

D   People did not have electricity to power the messages.

Part B: Which sentence from the passage **best** supports the answer in Part A?

A   "People could not send messages without wires."

B   "He tried using different metal shapes."

C   "They sent news about a boat race to New York newspapers."

D   "Radios were the messengers that brought news and music into homes across the world."

GO ON →

7 Complete the chart to show the effect of each cause. Mark **one** box next to **each** effect.

	Cause 1: Radio waves carry electric signals through the air.	**Cause 2:** Scientists believe radio waves cannot travel very far.
Effect: Marconi sends wireless signals from England to Canada.	☐	☐
Effect: Marconi runs tests sending wireless signals a mile away.	☐	☐

8 Read the sentence from the passage.

Marconi thought his <u>invention</u> could be used to send messages.

What is the root word of the word <u>invention</u>?

A vent

B invent

C tion

D inve

GO ON →

9 Read the sentence from the passage.

This meant that for a period of time he had the <u>right</u> to be the only one who could make or sell his product.

What does the word <u>right</u> mean in the sentence?

   A something to which one has a just claim

   B a set of actions for a ceremony

   C to make something correct

   D to form letters or words

10 What does the timeline help the reader understand about Marconi?

   A the places where Marconi lived

   B how his work led to Morse code

   C how he came up with his invention

   D the major events in Marconi's life

GO ON →

Read the passage. Then answer the questions.

Music for Everyone!

Music is everywhere. It can relax you or comfort you. It often makes you want to dance. There are many ways that music is valuable. Children need to have it in their lives. That is why students should be required to play a musical instrument starting in second grade.

Students can learn a great deal from playing a musical instrument. To begin with, it is an excellent way to use math skills. Music is not just about making sounds. It is made up of notes that are divided into fractions. A young musician must use math to learn how to keep a beat and stay in rhythm. Music really is the most creative way to practice math.

Students can also improve their coordination by playing a musical instrument. When you read music, your eyes send a signal to your brain, which sends a message to your hands. Your muscles then move to help create the right notes. Playing an instrument allows students to improve their reflexes and hand-eye coordination as a result.

Students can learn social skills with a musical instrument, as well. They often play different instruments in a band or orchestra. This allows them to work with classmates to play songs that blend sounds together. They learn the value of teamwork because they must each practice for the benefit of the entire group.

School officials would be wise to require students to play an instrument starting in second grade. Not everyone will be an amazing musician right away. However, learning and practicing a musical instrument will boost the spirit, mind, and body of all students.

Old MacDonald Had a Farm

Remembering even a simple combination of notes can improve your memory. Playing music is like an exercise for the brain.

GO ON →

11 The following question has two parts. First, answer part A. Then, answer part B.

Part A: What is the author's point of view about playing music?

A It is more important than other activities such as sports or clubs.

B It helps students learn how to do different things at once.

C It gives students a way to dance during school.

D It is the only way to teach children math skills.

Part B: Which sentence from the passage **best** supports the answer in Part A?

A "Music is everywhere."

B "It often makes you want to dance."

C "Students can learn a great deal from playing a musical instrument."

D "To begin with, it is an excellent way to use math skills."

12 Read the sentence from the passage.

There are many ways that music is <u>valuable</u>.

What does the word <u>valuable</u> mean?

A without value

B can be valued

C waiting to have value

D valued only sometimes

GO ON →

13 Circle the sentences from the passage that **best** show the author's point of view. Pick **two** choices.

"Children need to have it in their lives."

"It is made up of notes that are divided into fractions."

"A young musician must use math to learn how to keep a beat and stay in rhythm."

"When you read music, your eyes send a signal to your brain, which sends a message to your hands."

"Your muscles then move to help create the right notes."

"School officials would be wise to require students to play an instrument starting in second grade."

14 What does the caption under the photo help readers understand?

   A how music affects the memory

   B how songs are fun to sing

   C why sheet music can be confusing

   D why exercise is important

GO ON →

15   Read the sentence from the passage.

Music really is the most <u>creative</u> way to practice math.

What does the root word of <u>creative</u> mean? Pick **two** choices.

A   control

B   forget

C   make

D   build

E   sell

GO ON →

Read the passage below. Choose the word or words that correctly complete the sentences.

Last week, a fire broke out at an apartment building in ___(1)___ town. Luckily, there were no injuries. The firefighters came right away, and everyone got out of the building safely. But the fire destroyed seven apartments, and people lost all of their belongings.

Our teacher, Mr. Lachlan, told us about the fire. He ___(2)___ in that apartment building. Mr. Lachlan's apartment did not catch fire. But the people who lost their belongings are his neighbors.

Mr. Lachlan said, "Our class could start a project to help my neighbors. Does anyone have any ideas?"

Chara raised her hand and said, "I ___(3)___ some clothes that don't fit me anymore. Maybe ___(4)___ will fit your neighbors' children."

"I like your idea!" Mr. Lachlan told her. "We can collect books and toys for the children, too."

Then Mike said, "Let's have a bake sale to raise money. Mr. Lachlan's neighbors can use the money to replace furniture and other things ___(5)___ lost."

"Another good idea!" said Mr. Lachlan. "We'll do both of those things for our project."

GO ON →

16   Which answer should go in blank (1)?

    A   us

    B   ours

    C   our

    D   them

17   Which answer should go in blank (2)?

    A   live

    B   lives

    C   living

    D   will live

18   Which answer should go in blank (3)?

    A   have

    B   has

    C   having

    D   haved

GO ON →

19 Which answer should go in blank (4)?

    A them

    B their

    C they

    D they're

20 Which answer should go in blank (5)?

    A they's

    B theyve

    C them

    D they've

Informational Performance Task

Task:

Your class has been learning about different ways that people take action, such as protecting the earth by recycling. Now your class is going to create a website to share what they have learned. Each student will write an article for the website.

Before you decide what you will write about, you will read two sources that provide information on different ways people take action. After you have looked at these sources, you will answer some questions about them. Briefly scan the sources and the three questions that follow. Then, go back and read the sources carefully to gain the information you will need to answer the questions and write an informational article for the class website.

In Part 2, you will write your article using information from the two sources.

Directions for Part 1

You will now look at two sources. You can look at either of the sources as often as you like.

Research Questions:

After looking at the sources, use the rest of the time in Part 1 to answer three questions about them. Your answers to these questions will be scored. Also, your answers will help you think about the information you have read, which should help you write your informational article. You may refer to the sources when you think it would be helpful. You may also look at your notes.

GO ON →

Source #1: Farms Feed the World

America is a country rich in gifts from nature. Rivers and lakes give fresh water and fish. Forests have trees that can be made into many different things such as paper and houses. Oil and coal are used to make electricity and are found underground. But perhaps the greatest gift is the land itself. American farmers use the rich ground, called soil, to grow plants and to raise animals. They help to feed the people of the world.

America has been a country of farmers for a long time. Today there are over two million farms in the United States. Each of the 50 states has some type of farming.

The soil in which plants grow is a very important part of a farm. Soil is made of parts of plants and animals that are no longer living. It is also made of very tiny pieces of rock. As the dead plants and animals break down into smaller parts, they make the land better for growing new plants. Rich, healthy soil helps new plants get what they need to grow.

Farmers want to protect the land. They know that wind and water can destroy the soil. On a windy day, soil is picked up from fields and carried away. Water can make the loose soil wash away. Farmers use different ways to stop these things from happening. An example of this is a windbreak. Farmers plant a row of trees beside a field. The trees will stop, or break the wind from blowing away the loose soil. Farmers also know which plants to grow in areas where water may carry away the loose soil. The roots of these plants will help hold the soil in place.

Farmers have learned that, like living things, the land can lose some of its strength if it does not get rest. To help keep the soil strong, farmers may not grow anything in a field for one growing season. During that time, farmers may add non-living plant and animal parts to the soil. This will help make the soil rich for growing once again.

Because farmers know what a wonderful gift the soil is, they will continue to find new ways to keep it safe. There are many people all over the world who must be fed.

GO ON →

Source #2: American Forests

When America was first settled, almost half of the land was covered by forests. Today there are 155 national forests covering 8% of the United States. These forests are homes to many types of trees, plants, and animals.

The trees and plants of the forest give us many good things. They help make oxygen, which is a gas that we need to breathe. The leaves of the plants take in a harmful gas called carbon dioxide and change it into oxygen. The plants use carbon dioxide to make the food that they need to stay alive. It is a win-win situation for all living things!

The trees and the shade they make help to cool Earth. The ground under the shade of the trees does not get as hot as ground exposed to the sun. If the land is cool, the air above it is also cool. Forests all over Earth keep us from having terribly hot weather.

Scientists have studied the plants of the forest. They have found that parts of many plants may be used to help sick people. Medicines made from forest plants have been used for hundreds of years. Today scientists continue to discover new ways to use forest plants. They have found that the forest plants can be used to make items like soap and rubber.

The forest provides trees that have many purposes. Trees that are cut down can be used for building homes, items like tables and chairs, and even toys. Your homework paper and the napkin from the lunchroom most likely came from trees!

Hundreds of animals live in the forests of America. Bears, foxes, squirrels, and birds are a few animals that make their home in the forests. These creatures find what they need to stay alive in the tree-covered areas of our country. They eat plants or other small animals. They have safe places to raise their babies. But these animals also help the forest. Some carry seeds from one place to another. This helps new plants to grow in other areas of the forest.

GO ON →

To continue to enjoy all that forests provide, people must take care of the forests. A fire in a forest can cause terrible damage. Seventy years ago a group of people in the United States introduced Smokey the Bear. This character teaches people how to protect forests. Signs showing Smokey the Bear are placed by forests all over the United States. Smokey warns that fires in forests can destroy the homes of many animals. Over half of the forest fires that happen in the U.S. are started by people. This is why Smokey's message is so important.

GO ON →

Student Name _____

1   Choose **two** ideas that explain what **both** Source #1 and Source #2 say about what people get from nature.

   A   People breathe oxygen made by plants and trees.

   B   People cut trees to make many different items like paper and houses.

   C   People eat fish and drink fresh water that is found in rivers and lakes.

   D   Sick people are helped using the medicine made from plants.

   E   People use electricity made from oil and coal that is found underground.

   F   People are able to use many different things that nature gives.

2   The sources discuss the ways that people took action. Explain what the sources say about the ways that people took action. Use **one** detail from **each** source to support your explanation. For each detail, include the source title or number.

   _____

   _____

   _____

   _____

   _____

   _____

GO ON →

Copyright © McGraw-Hill Education

3 Each source explains why action was taken. Explain why it is important to take action. Use **one** example from Source #1 and **one** example from Source #2 to support your answer. For each example, include the source title or number.

_____

_____

_____

_____

_____

GO ON →

Directions for Part 2

You will now look at your sources, take notes, and plan, draft, revise, and edit your article for the website. First read your assignment and the information about how your informational article will be scored. Then begin your work.

Your Assignment:

Your class is creating a website about the ways that people can take action. For your part on the website, you have decided to write an informational article about people taking action. Your article will be read by other students, teachers, and parents.

Using more than one source, develop a main idea about people taking action. Choose the most important information from the sources to support your main idea. Then, write an informational article that is several paragraphs long. Clearly organize your article and support your main idea with details from the sources. Use your own words except when quoting directly from the sources. Be sure to give the source title or number when using details from the sources.

REMEMBER: A well-written informational article

- has a clear main idea
- is well-organized and stays on topic
- has an introduction and conclusion
- uses transitions
- uses details from the sources to support the main idea
- develops ideas fully
- uses clear language
- follows rules of writing (spelling, punctuation, and grammar)

Now begin work on your informational article. Manage your time carefully so that you can plan, write, revise, and edit the final draft of your informational article. Write your response on a separate sheet of paper.

Read the play. Then answer the questions.

Daedalus and Icarus

Characters

> KING MINOS
> DAEDALUS
> ICARUS

Scene 1

[*Setting: King Minos's castle on the island of Crete.*]

[*King Minos had asked Daedalus to design a maze to hold a monster. Daedalus eventually helped a young man, Theseus, who killed the monster and escaped the maze. King Minos's daughter has left the island with Theseus, her true love.*]

KING MINOS: Daedalus, you were my trusted inventor. How could you allow Theseus to escape the maze?

DAEDALUS: Your majesty, I never meant to betray your trust or to anger you. I only wanted to help the young man.

KING MINOS: [*Angered with Daedalus's response.*] You did more than help him! Because of your actions I will never see my daughter again. Guards, bring in the prisoner.

[*Two guards bring in Daedalus's son, Icarus.*]

DAEDALUS: [*Falls to the ground and bows to the king on his knees.*] No, King! I beg of you, please do not punish my son for my mistakes!

KING MINOS: Get up, you fool! You're barking up the wrong tree! No one tells me what to do. As punishment for your behavior, I banish you and your son, Icarus, to the maze. Take them away!

[*The guards remove the father and son.*]

GO ON →

Scene 2

[*Setting: Somewhere in the maze near the edge of the island.*]

DAEDALUS: I am upset that you did not listen and leave Crete after I helped Theseus.

ICARUS: I should have listened to you. Now we are trapped here forever!

DAEDALUS: Not forever! Last night, I came up with a plan. We will escape by air!

ICARUS: [*Confused with his father's suggestion.*] But Father, how will we do it? We would need wings.

DAEDALUS: [*Excited.*] You hit the nail on the head! I stayed up all night building us wings! I gathered twine and feathers and held them together using candle wax. I tested them, and they work!

ICARUS: That's amazing, Father!

DAEDALUS: But you must listen this time! Stay close to me and do not fly too high or too low. The spray from the waves will make the feathers stick together. The heat from the sun will cause the wax to melt.

[*Daedalus and Icarus put on their wings and begin to fly.*]

ICARUS: This is so much fun! [*He forgets his father's warning and soars higher and higher.*]

DAEDALUS: [*Shouting from far below.*] Stop! You're too high! Icarus!

[*The sun melts the wax and Icarus begins to fall. He realizes too late that he should have heeded his father's advice.*]

GO ON →

1 Read the stage directions from the play.

Two guards bring in Daedalus's son, Icarus.

How do the stage directions help the reader?

A They make the play scary.

B They make the play funny.

C They introduce a new character.

D They show what the characters think.

2 Underline **two** lines from the play that support the theme of the play.

"Because of your actions I will never see my daughter again."

"I beg of you, please do not punish my son for my mistakes!"

"I should have listened to you."

"Stay close to me and do not fly too high or too low."

"He realizes too late that he should have heeded his father's advice."

GO ON →

3 The following question has two parts. First, answer part A. Then, answer part B.

Part A: What would the play show if it was told from the point of view of Theseus?

    A why Icarus chose to stay on the island of Crete

    B why Daedalus decided to help Theseus escape

    C how Daedalus made the maze for the king

    D how Icarus was captured by King Minos

Part B: Which detail from the play **best** supports the answer in Part A?

    A "Daedalus eventually helped a young man, Theseus, who killed the monster and escaped the maze."

    B "I beg of you, please do not punish my son for my mistakes!"

    C "No one tells me what to do."

    D "Now we are trapped here forever!"

4 Read the line from the play.

You're barking up the wrong tree!

Why does King Minos say this line to Daedalus?

    A because Daedalus waits to tell the king his feelings

    B because Daedalus is upset that his son did not listen

    C because Daedalus is in a hurry to get away from the king

    D because Daedalus thinks he can change the king's mind

GO ON →

5   Read the lines from the play.

You <u>hit the nail on the head</u>! I stayed up all night building us wings!

What do the words "hit the nail on the head" mean?

   A to miss a chance

   B to work very hard

   C to say something exactly right

   D to believe someone without proof

GO ON →

Read the passage. Then answer the questions.

The Ant Man

If you want to know something about ants, ask the famous teacher and writer Dr. Edward O. Wilson. He has been watching ants since he was a boy in the 1930s. His books *The Ants* and *On Human Nature* won Pulitzer prizes.

His Early Life

At first, Wilson was interested in birds. Bird watchers need sharp eyes and ears. As a boy, he hurt one eye and then lost some of his hearing. He knew then that he had to study something else. Wilson began watching ants. He spent a lot of time crawling on his hands and knees, following ants to their nests. He would then inspect the nests to see what the ants were doing.

Social Animals

Dr. Wilson thinks we can learn from ants and other social animals, such as bees. Social animals live and work together. They share work, food, and information. In addition to those behaviors, they also keep each other safe. People are social animals, too.

Most ants live in nests they make from soil, wood, or leaves, while some live in trees or hollow plant stems. Ants in a nest have specific, or special, jobs. The queen lays eggs. The workers collect food for the queen and the other ants. Some workers take care of the queen's eggs, while others keep the nest clean for the entire colony, or group, of ants. Soldier ants fight off and attack other ants that threaten the colony.

All Kinds of Ants

Ants are everywhere. Hot places like Central America have the most species, or different kinds, of ants. One kind is the harvester ant. Harvester ants bring grass, seeds, and berries into their nests. Everyone shares the food that has been collected.

GO ON →

Other ant species do work similar to farming. Honey ants eat honeydew, a sweet liquid that aphids make. Aphids are small insects that suck juices from plants. Honey ants stroke an aphid's belly until honeydew comes out. This method of gathering the honeydew imitates the process humans use to get milk from cows.

Not only do ants use their eyes to find their way home, they also use their noses. Dr. Wilson found that ants communicate with each other through smells. When one ant senses danger, it gives off an odor. The other ants smell it and make the same odor. Soon the whole nest knows there is danger. Then they can hide or run away.

Learning About Nature

A person who studies insects is good with details. But Dr. Wilson can see the big picture, too. He worries that many plant and animal species are becoming extinct or dying off. Each species plays a part in the natural world. Once a species is gone, there is no way to replace it.

The plants and animals in nature help people in many ways. They clean water and make the soil in which we grow food. They even make the air we breathe. According to Dr. Wilson, "By destroying nature, we are throwing away a gift."

But Dr. Wilson thinks people have stopped doing some of the things that hurt the natural world. We are respecting nature a little more than before. The more we learn about nature, the more we want to conserve or protect it.

GO ON →

6 What did Wilson do when he couldn't study birds anymore?

    A He became interested in ants.

    B He went to different doctors.

    C He wrote books on birds he researched.

    D He spent most of his time staying home.

7 Read the sentence from the passage.

He would then <u>inspect</u> the nests to see what the ants were doing.

<u>Inspect</u> has the Latin root -*spect,* which means "watch or look." What does <u>inspect</u> mean?

    A look quickly

    B look carefully

    C watch for changes

    D watch for a long time

8 The following question has two parts. First, answer part A. Then, answer part B.

Part A: How do ants know that something dangerous is happening?

    A They fight other ants.

    B They stroke the belly of an aphid.

    C They smell an odor that tells them to run.

    D They hide when they know they are being watched.

GO ON →

Part B: Which sentence **best** supports the answer in Part A?

A "Wilson began watching ants."

B "Soldier ants fight off and attack other ants that threaten the colony."

C "Aphids are small insects that suck juices from plants."

D "When one ant senses danger, it gives off an odor."

9   Complete the chart to show the problem and solution in the passage. Mark **one** box under the problem and solution.

	Problem	Solution
Ants are social animals that share everything.	☐	☐
People can learn to care about nature.	☐	☐
Many animals and plants are dying off.	☐	☐

10   Read the sentence from the passage.

Everyone shares the food that has been <u>collected</u>.

What does the root word of <u>collected</u> mean? Pick **two** choices.

A try

B eat

C get

D make

E gather

GO ON →

Read the poem. Then answer the questions.

Out of This World

All through the afternoon, Luis and I were in my room
Cocooned with our computer games. Then Mom
Appeared and asked, "Do you two even know it's summer?
Go run around, play tag, do something!"
5   But when I tried to walk,
I stumbled. My legs had gone to sleep!
"Okay, we need to move," I said.
Just then the news came on.

"A lunar eclipse," the newsman said.
10   "The moon will hide its face!"
He sure did seem excited, but I didn't understand.
I asked my mom, "Eclipse—what's that? I never heard of it."
"It happens when the Earth, the moon, and sun line up.
The moon goes through our Earth's shadow,
15   And it's very strange to see.
I know a place to see it from. Shall we go out and watch?"

Luis and I both wanted to, and so when evening came,
The three of us got on the train and rode out to the end.
We walked and walked. The sun went down,
20   The moon came up and peeked above a hill,
Where people sat just waiting for the show.
The full moon climbed up high and higher
As we sat in its bright glow.

GO ON →

We were all bathed in light almost as bright as day.
25 I said, "Hey, look, I see my shadow!" and then I jumped up high.
We danced and watched our shadows stretch out far behind us.
Then someone said, "It's starting now,"
And everyone looked up.
A curving, fuzzy shadow crept across the big, bright moon.
30 Behind the curve, the moon's face became a smoky orange.

The spectators grew quiet as the moon turned almost black.
How strange it was to think that Earth
Could block off all that light.
And then Luis jumped up and started waving both his arms.
35 I said to him, "Luis, my friend, what are you doing now?"
"An astronaut just waved at me!" he joked.
But then he laughed.
"Ha-ha, I'm just pulling your leg," he said.
"This moon is making me silly!"

40 Earth's shadow slipped away and then—our bright full
moon was back!
We oohed and aahed and cheered out loud. I felt
so glad to be a part of this big crowd cheering for the moon.
Just think, I would have missed it if I'd stayed in my room.
45 And later on the train home, I watched the moon sail on
so cold and white, so high, with us down here on Earth.

GO ON →

11 In the first stanza, why does the narrator need to get up and move? Pick **two** choices.

    A The narrator feels unhealthy.

    B The narrator's legs go numb.

    C The narrator is getting tired from hard work.

    D The narrator is falling asleep at the computer.

    E The narrator's body is tired from not being used.

12 Read the lines below. Circle the word that helps you figure out the meaning of "pulling your leg."

And then Luis jumped up and started waving both his arms.

I said to him, "Luis, my friend, what are you doing now?"

"An astronaut just waved at me!" he joked.

But then he laughed.

"Ha-ha, I'm just <u>pulling your leg</u>," he said.

13 The following question has two parts. First, answer part A. Then, answer part B.

Part A: Which sentence **best** tells the theme of the poem?

    A If you don't go outside, you will miss amazing things.

    B If you don't dance, you might forget to have fun.

    C The moon looks brighter from some places.

    D Eclipses do not happen often.

GO ON →

Part B: Which line from the poem **best** supports the answer in Part A?

A   "'It happens when the Earth, the moon, and sun line up.'"

B   "We were all bathed in light almost as bright as day."

C   "We danced and watched our shadows stretch out far behind us."

D   "Just think, I would have missed it if I'd stayed in my room."

14   How does the narrator feel about the eclipse? Support your answer with details from the poem.

_____

_____

_____

_____

_____

GO ON →

15 Read the line from the poem.

"An <u>astronaut</u> just waved at me!" he said.

The Greek root *astro* means "star" and the root *naut* means "sailor or ship." What does <u>astronaut</u> mean?

A   a pirate ship

B   a star in the solar system

C   a traveler in a spacecraft

D   a person who studies ships

GO ON →

Read the passage below. Choose the word or words that correctly complete the sentences.

Isabel and I were walking to the park on a burning hot day. The heat came up from the sidewalk ___(1)___ our feet. We decided to see who could run ___(2)___ than the other. We were already soaked, so it didn't matter if we got even ___(3)___ . We ran until Isabel stopped and begged me to buy her some lemonade.

"You just had a giant glass of water at home," I said. "As soon as you're splashing around in the fountain, you'll be as cool as a cucumber."

We walked ___(4)___ the avenue where all the stores were. Mr. Kim's sidewalk fruit stand was piled high with fruit, vegetables, and ice. I asked him if we could have some ice from his display.

He said, "Sure, but not too much. I've got to keep all ___(5)___ food cool."

I rubbed the ice on my neck. It melted quickly and made me feel better. Isabel said, "We'll be at the park soon. Hopefully it's cooler there."

GO ON →

16 Which answer should go in blank (1)?

    A from

    B under

    C with

    D in

17 Which answer should go in blank (2)?

    A fast

    B fasts

    C fastest

    D faster

18 Which answer should go in blank (3)?

    A sweatier

    B sweatiest

    C sweaty

    D sweat

GO ON →

19 Which answer should go in blank (4)?

    A during

    B over

    C to

    D for

20 Which answer should go in blank (5)?

    A these

    B this

    C those

    D them

Opinion Performance Task

Task:

Your class has been learning about how people decide what is important. Your class discussions have focused on how people make important decisions such as which school club to join or what clothes to wear based on the weather. Now your teacher is going to create a display board outside of your classroom to share what the class has learned about making important decisions. Each student will write a paper for the board.

Before you decide what you will write about, you will read two sources that provide information on how people decide what is important. After you have looked at these sources, you will answer some questions about them. Briefly scan the sources and the three questions that follow. Then, go back and read the sources carefully to gain the information you will need to answer the questions and write an opinion paper for the class's display board.

In Part 2, you will write your paper using information from the two sources.

Directions for Part 1

You will now look at two sources. You can look at either of the sources as often as you like.

Research Questions:

After looking at the sources, use the rest of the time in Part 1 to answer three questions about them. Your answers to these questions will be scored. Also, your answers will help you think about the information you have read, which should help you write your opinion paper. You may refer to the sources when you think it would be helpful. You may also look at your notes.

GO ON →

Source #1: Why Save Libraries?

Where can you surf the internet, read a book, join a reading club, and borrow a video game, mostly for free? Your local library, of course!

Libraries do lots of good things for their communities. Unfortunately, libraries all over the country are being forced to close. Many of them are facing funding cuts and no longer have the money to stay open, let alone add to their services. With more people downloading e-books to read on tablets and computers, many people wonder how important libraries still are. Should they stay open?

Actually, libraries do a lot more than lend books. Libraries usually have computers available for public use. Libraries are quiet places to study and work. And, if a question comes up while you're working, librarians will be happy to help you find the answer. If you want to research almost any topic—from dinosaurs to ancient Egypt—just ask a librarian!

Public libraries usually include a section just for children. Here, you can find books, magazines, and movies especially for kids. You might be surprised to know that many libraries also loan video games and even toys. "Story time" is popular with younger and older children alike. Do you love comic books or mysteries? Many libraries host clubs based on popular books so you can meet others who share your interests, too.

Did you know that libraries can help you succeed in school? Libraries often have reading tutor programs. Studies show that these types of programs greatly improve the ability of children to read and write. These same services are made available to adults as well.

And of course, libraries still do loan books. Most public libraries have the latest best sellers, as well as many other lesser-known titles. Librarians can help steer you to new and interesting books that you might otherwise miss. Based on your interests, a librarian can open the door to many new, enjoyable books.

These are just a few of the many important roles libraries play in a healthy community. A library is a world of wonder, just waiting for you to open the door and discover what's inside. If a library is forced to close its doors, the whole community loses a valuable resource.

GO ON →

Source #2: Saving Memories

Have you ever wanted to save memories of a special trip or activity? Your first thought might be to take photos or a video. These are great ways to remember special times. But, there are lots of other clever ways to save your memories.

Shadow Boxes

Shadow boxes were first created by sailors. When a sailor retires and is leaving the ship for the last time, it is believed to be bad luck for his or her shadow to touch land before he or she does. To avoid this from happening, sailors would use a wooden box to display items of importance to the person retiring.

You can create your own shadow box to display small items you want to remember. Choose some small objects that you collected on a trip. You could also choose some favorite pieces from a collection. Glue the items inside the box and hang it up on a wall or keep it on a bookshelf.

Scrapbooks

Scrapbook pages are a great way to keep memories of events. If you want to remember a school play, you could choose photos, tickets, and posters to glue on the scrapbook page. Once your page is done, keep it in a big scrapbook. Each page you add to the book means more saved memories.

Creating scrapbooks has become very popular. There are scrapbooking groups in towns and online as well as books on this activity. If you want ideas on how to start your scrapbooking, there are many sources that can help you.

Quilting

You can even save memories of your favorite clothes! When you outgrow your favorite jeans or t-shirts, you can have them made into a quilt. Some women have used part of their wedding dresses in quilts! Cutting the clothes and creating a quilt would be a keepsake you could have for many years.

GO ON →

For hundreds of years, people have quilted to create memories. Quilts usually last a long time and can be handed down from one group of family members to another. It is not unheard of to have a quilt that was made by someone's great-great grandmother for example.

There are many creative ways to save memories and these are just a few. No matter what you choose, it will be unique because the memories behind what you've made are yours.

GO ON →

Source #3: Time Capsules

Time Capsules

What is a Time Capsule?

- A time capsule is a container of different things that tell about the time in which it is made.

- Time capsules are usually buried, to be opened at some point in the future.

- Time capsules often contain everyday items, such as photos, toys, and tools.

- They also hold writings, such as letters, articles, and advertisements.

GO ON →

What's Inside a Time Capsule?

Include a drawing that shows what a typical time capsule could look like, labeling the parts:

— Waterproof container

— Everyday objects (could include toys, cards, coins, etc.)

— Magazine article

— Photo

— Etc.

Paul Revere's Time Capsule

• In 1795, Paul Revere and Samuel Adams buried a time capsule in the Massachusetts State House in Boston.

• Historians had to remove the time capsule in 2014 due to a water leak in the building.

• The time capsule likely contains a plate, coins, and texts from the 1600s.

GO ON →

Other Time Capsules

- The Detroit Century Box was buried December 31, 1900 and opened on the same day in 2000. It contained photographs and letters from Detroit residents with predictions for the future.

- The 1939 World's Fair time capsule weighs 800 pounds and contains seeds, a microscope, news film and a catalog, among other things. It is meant to be opened in 6939.

- The KEO satellite will carry messages from Earth's inhabitants. The plan is to launch it into space and have it return to Earth in 50,000 years.

How to Make a Time Capsule

You will need:

- A waterproof container (such as a glass jar with tight-fitting lid)

- Items that show what is important to you (favorite toys, things you use every day)

- Writings that tell about you and your life (books, magazine articles, journals)

- A label for the outside of the container (tell what it is and when it should be opened)

Simply place the items in the container and close the lid. You could bury the container or store it with instructions for opening.

Note: Be sure to get your parents' permission before creating the time capsule!

GO ON →

What to Put Inside a Time Capsule

Some things to think about when making a time capsule:

- Don't include things that can break down or rot over time, such as food or liquids.

- All of the items should be dry. Water can create mold and destroy items over time.

- If you want to include clothing, polyester material is least likely to break down.

GO ON →

1   What do **both** Source #1 and the presentation about time
     capsules say about saving what is important? Pick **two** choices.

   A   Not everyone thinks it is important to save certain things.

   B   Sometimes it costs money to save things that are important.

   C   People can take action to save what they think is important.

   D   The community could be affected if important resources are
       not saved.

   E   Saving what is important can lead to a discovery of new
       information.

   F   It takes too long to see the reward that comes with saving
       what is important.

2   Explain what the sources say about how people can save what is
     important to them. Use **one** detail from Source #2 and **one** detail
     from the presentation to support your explanation. For each detail,
     include the source title or number.

     _____

     _____

     _____

     _____

     _____

     _____

GO ON →

3   Explain why people choose to save what is important to them. Give
two reasons, one from Source #1 and one from the presentation to
support your explanation. For each reason, include the source title
or number.

_____

_____

_____

_____

_____

GO ON →

Directions for Part 2

You will now look at your sources, take notes, and plan, draft, revise, and edit your paper for the display board. First read your assignment and the information about how your opinion paper will be scored. Then begin your work.

Your Assignment:

Your teacher is putting up a display board outside of your classroom. The board will show all that your class has learned about how people decide what is important. You have decided to write an opinion paper that is several paragraphs long about deciding what is important. Based on the information in the sources, write an opinion paper on if you agree or disagree that it is important to save items from the past. The paper will be read by other students, teachers, parents.

Make sure you clearly state your opinion and write several paragraphs supporting your opinion with reasons and details from the sources. Develop your ideas clearly and use your own words, except when quoting directly from the sources. Be sure to give the source title or number for the details or facts you use.

REMEMBER: A well-written opinion paper

- has a clear opinion
- is well-organized and stays on topic
- has an introduction and conclusion
- uses transitions
- uses details or facts from the sources to support the opinion
- puts the information from the sources in quotes when necessary
- gives the title or number of the source for the details or facts included
- develops ideas clearly
- uses clear language
- follows rules of writing (spelling, punctuation, and grammar)

Now begin work on your opinion paper. Manage your time carefully so that you can plan, write, revise, and edit the final draft of your opinion paper. Write your response on a separate sheet of paper.

Copyright © McGraw-Hill Education

Unit 1 Answer Key

Student Name: _____

Question	Correct Answer	Content Focus	Complexity
1	B	Character, Setting, Plot: Sequence	DOK 2
2A	A	Character, Setting, Plot: Sequence	DOK 2
2B	D	Character, Setting, Plot: Sequence / Text Evidence	DOK 2
3	D	Multiple-Meaning Words	DOK 2
4	C, F	Character, Setting, Plot: Sequence	DOK 2
5	see below	Compound Words	DOK 1
6	A, C	Context Clues: Synonyms	DOK 2
7A	C	Main Idea and Key Details	DOK 2
7B	D	Main Idea and Key Details/Text Evidence	DOK 2
8	see below	Text Features: Maps	DOK 2
9	C	Text Structure: Sequence	DOK 3
10	B	Compound Words	DOK 1
11	see below	Text Features: Headings	DOK 2
12A	A	Main Idea and Key Details	DOK 2
12B	B	Main Idea and Key Details/Text Evidence	DOK 2
13	B, D	Context Clues: Synonyms	DOK 2
14	D	Multiple-Meaning Words	DOK 2
15	A	Text Features: Sidebars/Headings	DOK 2
16	B	Sentences and Sentence Fragments	DOK 1
17	A	Simple and Compound Sentences	DOK 1
18	C	Sentences	DOK 1
19	A	Commands and Exclamations	DOK 1
20	C	Commands and Exclamations	DOK 1

Comprehension 1, 2A, 2B, 4, 7A, 7B, 8, 9, 11, 12A, 12B, 15	/18	%
Vocabulary 3, 5, 6, 10, 13, 14	/12	%
English Language Conventions 16, 17, 18, 19, 20	/5	%
Total Unit 1 Assessment Score	/35	%

5   Student should circle the following word:
- birthday

8   **2-point response:** The map shows that an oil well exploded in the Gulf of Mexico and caused an oil spill. This oil spill affected beaches in four states—Louisiana, Mississippi, Alabama, and Florida.

11   Students should match the following:
- The day and time don't matter. — When Do You Do It?
- It creates great memories. — Why Should You Do It?
- Families choose the activity. — What Is Family Time?
- Some kids live with grandparents. — Who Is Invited?

Narrative Performance Task			
Question	Answer	Complexity	Score
1	see below	DOK 2	/1
2	see below	DOK 3	/2
3	see below	DOK 3	/2
Story	see below	DOK 4	/4 [P/O] /4 [D/E] /2 [C]
Total Score			/15

1 • Source #1: Living History
   - Visiting old places can help people understand history.
   • Source #2: A Visit to the Natural History Museum
   - Viewing collections of things from the past is one way to learn about history.

2 **2-point response:** Source #1 and Source #2 tell about different ways to learn about the past. One thing people can learn by visiting an old place is to understand what life was really like long ago. For instance, visiting Columbia, California, helps people imagine what it was like to live in the 1850s and look for gold. One thing people can learn by visiting a natural history museum is all about the history and nature of people who lived long ago. If you go to the dinosaur room in a museum, you can see the bones and skeletons of these animals. You can also learn lots of different facts about how they lived. Both sources are important for understanding important histories.

3 **2-point response:** Source #1 and Source #2 show that it is important to understand the past. In Source #1, visiting these towns that are part of our country's past helps us understand how people used to live. It is important to learn about these things because we see how life has changed for people. Going to Native American pueblos helps us see what it was like to live there. In Source #2, it is easy to visit museums since many cities and towns have one. Museums are important because of all the different things you can learn in one place. You can learn about jewelry in one part and Egyptian tombs in another part. You can learn about many different parts of the past, so you get a larger idea of our history.

10-point anchor paper: When we finally got to the natural history museum we were greeted by a woman named Abigail. She was dressed like a pioneer woman and said she was from the 1800s! She told us about how she makes candles and even showed how she does it. She told us that her husband was a hat maker, and he came out of his shop to show us one of the hats he was making.

After that we went to a different part of the museum. There weren't any people dressed up in this room but there were "living" creatures – dinosaurs! The dinosaur room of the museum had a huge Tyrannosaurus Rex that came to life and roared every few minutes. There were plants all around him, and a museum guide told us those were the types of plants the other dinosaurs would eat. We were able to see the bones of some of those dinosaurs.

Once we left the dinosaur room, we entered the Native American room, and we were greeted by a man named Hania. He showed us the tools he used to build his home, which is called a pueblo. His home was made of mud to keep out the heat of the desert where he lived. He also showed us the weapons he used when he went hunting.

My favorite display was when we went to the gem room. It was like going into a jewelry store from the past! This room had beautiful diamonds and rubies within the glass cases. I understand why they protected this room with the glass cases because everything was breathtaking. I wish I could have stayed in there longer, but soon it was time to go.

I really had a great time at the museum of natural history. I was able to talk to people from the past and see animals and objects from long ago too. Seeing history with my own eyes meant so much to me, and it was a great way to learn more about history.

Unit 1 Rationales

1

A is incorrect because Jayden sees kids playing soccer in the park after he watches classmates in the playground.

B is correct Jayden watches his classmates playing in the playground at the very beginning of the passage.

C is incorrect because Jayden goes to his neighbor's backyard after the events listed in all the other choices.

D is incorrect because Jayden walks home from school after he watches his classmates in the playground.

2A

A is correct because Jayden realizes his mistake at night when he thinks about how Barry shared his toy with Ava.

B is incorrect because Jayden does not realize his mistake until after he gets his mother's note and walks over to his neighbor's backyard.

C is incorrect because Jayden does not realize his mistake until after he sees how Barry plays with Ava at his neighbor's house.

D is incorrect because Jayden has already realized his mistake before he approaches Tyler in the playground.

2B

A is incorrect because the sentence doesn't show Jayden realizing his mistake.

B is incorrect because the sentence doesn't show Jayden realizing his mistake.

C is incorrect because the sentence doesn't show Jayden realizing his mistake.

D is correct because Jayden realizes that he learned something from his brother: how to make friends and how he's been going about it the wrong way.

3

A is incorrect because the word *roll* is used as a verb to show movement.

B is incorrect because the word *roll* is used as a verb in the sentence.

C is incorrect because the word *roll* is used to show movement, but Ava is not turning the car over and over.

D is correct because the word *roll* is used to show that Ava is moving the car using its wheels.

4

A is incorrect because there is no evidence showing Jayden feeling embarrassed at the end.

B is incorrect because there is no evidence showing Jayden feeling confused at the end.

C is correct because Jayden says "sure!" to playing soccer and feels excited to make new friends.

D is incorrect because there is no evidence showing Jayden feeling tired at the end.

E is incorrect because there is no evidence showing Jayden feeling angry at the end.

F is correct because Jayden specifies the position he plays and feels hopeful in continuing to play soccer with these new friends.

5

The word *birthday* is the compound word, and it is made up of the words *birth* and *day*.

6

A is correct because the words "layer of oil" suggest that sludge is a slimy or dirty mixture.

B is incorrect because there is no evidence suggesting that sludge means "soapy water."

C is correct because the words "layer of oil" suggest that sludge is a slimy or dirty mixture.

D is incorrect because there is no evidence suggesting that sludge means "feathers."

E is incorrect because there is no evidence suggesting that sludge means "weeds."

7A

A is incorrect because this is a detail in the passage; it is not the main idea.

B is incorrect because the rescue of the pelican is not the focus of the entire passage.

C is correct because all of the ideas in the passage support this main idea.

D is incorrect because this detail is part of a larger idea presented in the passage.

7B

A is incorrect because this sentence supports a detail about the pelican and not the main idea.

B is incorrect because this sentence supports a detail about the oil wells and not the main idea.

C is incorrect because this sentence supports a detail about the other animals in the rescue center and not the main idea.

D is correct because the boat continuing to search for animals supports the main idea that the rescuers are trying to help all the animals affected by the spill.

8

See answer key for sample response.

9

A is incorrect because the passage does not offer a new solution to save the animals in the Gulf, but rather tells about the best solution that volunteers could provide at the time.

B is incorrect because the passage discusses the efforts of many volunteers; it does not list the many effects of a single volunteer.

C is correct because the passage retells what happened immediately following the oil spill in the Gulf of Mexico and then three months later.

D is incorrect because the passage does not compare the Gulf oil spill to any other oil spills in history.

10

A is incorrect because the words in the compound word *shoreline* suggest that land and water are involved.

B is correct because the words *shore* and *line* indicate that it is where water meets land.

C is incorrect because the word *shoreline* relates to water and land, not a boat.

D is incorrect because the words *shore* and *line* refer to where water meets land.

11

The following correct matches indicate the details found in each section of the passage:

The day and time don't matter. — When Do You Do It?

It creates great memories. — Why Should You Do It?

Families choose the activity. — What Is Family Time?

Some kids live with grandparents. — Who Is Invited?

12A

A is correct because the main idea of the passage is how family time is important for connecting with family.

B is incorrect because this is a detail about families being large.

C is incorrect because this is a detail about how busy people are these days.

D is incorrect because this is not a detail in the passage.

12B

A is incorrect because this is a detail in the passage; it does not support the main idea.

B is correct because all of the ideas in the passage support this main idea.

C is incorrect because this detail is not the main focus of the entire passage.

D is incorrect because this detail is part of a larger idea presented in the passage.

13

A is incorrect because "go out" doesn't give a clue to the meaning of "schedule."

B is correct because "every Sunday" suggests a routine and following a schedule.

C is incorrect because "often choose" doesn't give a clue to the meaning of "schedule."

D is correct because "a time" suggests when an event might take place or be scheduled.

E is incorrect because "based on" doesn't give a clue to the meaning of "schedule."

14

A is incorrect because the word *close* does not mean confined or having a tight space in the sentence.

B is incorrect because the word *close* does not mean that something is about to happen in the sense of time in the sentence.

C is incorrect because the word *close* does not mean physically close in terms of distance in the sentence.

D is correct because the word *close* means feeling connected in terms of feelings and emotions in the sentence.

15

A is correct because the sidebar provides examples of family time activities, which are referred to in the section under "What Is Family Time?"

B is incorrect because the section under "When Do You Do It?" refers to when family time takes place, and the sidebar refers to types of family time activities.

C is incorrect because the activities in the sidebar are not referenced in the section under "Who Is Invited?"

D is incorrect because the section under "Why Should You Do It?" explains why it is helpful to have family time, not activities to do together.

16

A is incorrect because the sentence contains the subject *parents* and the verb *took* to form a complete sentence.

B is correct because the sentence is missing a verb making the sentence incomplete.

C is incorrect because the sentence contains the subject *cat* and the verb *raised* to form a complete sentence.

D is incorrect because the sentence contains the subject *she* and the verb *likes* to form a complete sentence.

17

A is correct because the conjunction *but* fixes the run-on sentence and clarifies the meaning of the sentence.

B is incorrect because the conjunction *so* changes the meaning of the sentence.

C is incorrect because the conjunction *or* changes the meaning of the sentence.

D is incorrect because the sentence is missing a coordinating conjunction and does not fix the run-on sentence.

18

A is incorrect because "how" is the start of the sentence and should be capitalized; the sentence should also end with a question mark.

B is incorrect because the sentence should end with a question mark, not an exclamation mark.

C is correct because "How" is properly capitalized and the sentence ends with a question mark.

D is incorrect because "how" is the start of the sentence and should be capitalized.

19

A is correct because the sentence provides a directive telling the audience to "think about it."

B is incorrect because the sentence is descriptive and does not provide direction.

C is incorrect because the sentence is descriptive and does not provide direction.

D is incorrect because the sentence is descriptive and does not provide direction.

20

A is incorrect because the sentence should not be missing a quotation mark.

B is incorrect because the sentence should end with some sort of punctuation, not a comma.

C is correct because the sentence is exclamatory.

D is incorrect because the sentence is not a question.

Student Name: _____

Question	Correct Answer	Content Focus	Complexity
1	see below	Literary Elements: Illustrations	DOK 2
2	D, F	Figurative Language: Similes	DOK 2
3A	D	Theme	DOK 3
3B	B	Theme/ Text Evidence	DOK 3
4	see below	Theme	DOK 3
5	C	Figurative Language: Similes	DOK 2
6A	B	Author's Point of View	DOK 3
6B	D	Author's Point of View/ Text Evidence	DOK 3
7	C	Prefixes: un-	DOK 1
8	A, E	Author's Point of View	DOK 3
9	see below	Prefixes: un-	DOK 1
10	B	Author's Point of View	DOK 3
11	D	Rhyme	DOK 1
12	C	Figurative Language: Similes	DOK 2
13	see below	Alliteration	DOK 1
14A	A	Point of View	DOK 2
14B	D	Point of View/ Text Evidence	DOK 2
15	C, E	Figurative Language: Similes	DOK 2
16	B	Kinds of Nouns	DOK 1
17	D	Possessive Nouns	DOK 1
18	C	Combining Sentences	DOK 1
19	A	Irregular Plural Nouns	DOK 1
20	B	Singular and Plural Nouns	DOK 1

Unit 2 Answer Key

Student Name: _____

Comprehension 1, 3A, 3B, 4, 6A, 6B, 8, 10, 11, 13, 14A, 14B	/18	%
Vocabulary 2, 5, 7, 9, 12, 15	/12	%
English Language Conventions 16, 17, 18, 19, 20	/5	%
Total Unit 2 Assessment Score	/35	%

1   Students should underline the following details:
- The illustration shows how crowded it is on the ship.
- The illustration shows how Liam and his mum look happy.

4   **2-point response:** In the story "Leaving Ireland Behind," Liam and his mother are on a long voyage from Ireland to America. Liam is excited to move to New York and be with his father, who has been living there for two years. When they reach America, Liam finally gets to hug his father, showing that family is where the heart is.

9   Students should match the following:
- The meaning of unusual – strange
- Uses the prefix *un-* like unusual – untrue

13   Students should circle the following words:
- spring
- sing
- softly

Informational Performance Task

Question	Answer	Complexity	Score
1	see below	DOK 2	/1
2	see below	DOK 3	/2
3	see below	DOK 3	/2
Article	see below	DOK 4	/4 [P/O] /4 [E/E] /2 [C]
Total Score			**/15**

1 • Source #1: A Holiday for Trees
    - Using a good idea can help people set an example in their own lives.
  • Source #2: Searching for Lost Treasure
    - Asking people for help is sometimes needed when solving a problem.
  • Both Source #1 and Source #2
    - Reaching a goal as an adult can start from something that happened during one's childhood.

2 **2-point response:** If Morton and Clifford did not have a plan, then they would not have been able to reach their goals. In Source #1, it says that Morton wanted to share his love of trees with other people. He began to write newspaper articles about the trees that he brought back to his house. Without a plan to share his love of trees, others may not have read about and learned to care for trees. In Source #2, it says that Clifford looked up more information at the library about the ship. The maps that Clifford studied showed him where to look for the treasure. Without a plan, Clifford would not have known the best place to look to find the treasure.

3 **2-point response:** The work of Morton and Clifford gave others new information about things that they did not already know. Source #1 says that by reading Morton's stories about trees, people learned how trees could help them. The Arbor Day holiday was started because of Morton's work. Now people all over the world celebrate the importance of trees. Source #2 says that Clifford's crew found items like spoons, pens, and tools on the ship. Because of the items that the crew found, people had a better understanding of the way the pirates lived their lives. Also, because Clifford put the treasure that he found in a museum, many other people are now able to learn what life was like for pirates.

Unit 2 Answer Key

10-point anchor paper: In order to solve a problem, you must be determined and have a plan to solve the problem. Both of the men mentioned in the sources do these things and are able to solve their problems successfully.

In "A Holiday for Trees" Morton wants to see more trees where he lives. The article says that at the time Nebraska was called "the Great American Desert" and few trees were there. He decided to plant trees at his house and then he wrote about all of the good things trees can do for people. He eventually was able to share his love of trees with others, and the entire state started planting more trees. Morton's plan was to share his love of trees, and that's what he did.

In "Searching for Lost Treasure," Clifford wanted to find a sunken pirate ship. He solved his problem by planning as well. He did years of research reading about the ship that he wanted to find. He then gathered a crew and started the search. They kept looking for the treasure even though they wanted to give up. Clifford's determination and good planning led him to finally finding the treasure. Instead of selling his treasure, he donated it to a museum so other people could see it and enjoy it.

Both men in the articles had a strong determination to solve their problems. Morton solved his problem by planting trees of his own and getting others to plant trees too. Clifford solved his problem of wanting to find the treasure by doing research and not giving up. Both men solved their problems and shared their joy with others.

Unit 2 Rationales

1

Students should underline the details that explain how the ship is crowded and uncomfortable and how Liam and his mother are excited and happy to get off the boat and arrive at New York.

2

A is incorrect because the simile does not evoke a calm mood for Liam, the narrator.

B is incorrect because the simile does not show how Liam feels silly seeing his father.

C is incorrect because the simile does not evoke a funny mood.

D is correct because the simile shows how Liam is full of joy at the thought of seeing his father.

E is incorrect because the simile does not evoke a relaxed mood for Liam.

F is correct because the simile shows how Liam is in a cheerful mood to see his father.

3A

A is incorrect because there is no evidence in the passage showing the characters making mistakes.

B is incorrect because while Liam makes new friends on the ship, that detail is not the main theme of the passage.

C is incorrect because while Liam and his mother are kind people, that is not the main theme of the passage.

D is correct because the passage explains that Liam and his mother are travelling to New York to make a new and better life for their family.

3B

A is incorrect because this sentence does not support the theme of new beginnings bringing new promise.

B is correct because this sentence supports the theme of new beginnings bringing new promise.

C is incorrect because this sentence is a detail about Liam's father working hard and saving money.

D is incorrect because this sentence is a detail about Liam's friends.

4

See answer key for sample response.

5

A is incorrect because there is no evidence in the passage that the dad is excited to travel anywhere.

B is incorrect because there is no evidence that the dad wants to go swimming.

C is correct because the dad's smile is large as his family runs to hug him, showing that he is happy.

D is incorrect because the dad never says anything about wanting to go on the boat.

6A

A is incorrect because the author appreciates the scientists and the work they do to help the puffins.

B is correct because the author writes about the efforts of Kress and the scientists with admiration and in the end is thankful to have the birds return to Maine.

C is incorrect because the author doesn't talk about bringing back other animals.

D is incorrect because this opinion is never stated in the passage.

6B

A is incorrect because this is a detail that does not support the author's point of view.

B is incorrect because this is a detail that does not support the author's point of view.

C is incorrect because this is a detail that does not support the author's point of view.

D is correct because "thanks to their efforts" shows how the author is happy to have the puffin back in America.

7

A is incorrect because the prefix *un-* means "not" so "unharmed" means to be kept out of harm, not "bothered."

B is incorrect because "unharmed" does not mean "careful."

C is correct because "unharmed" means "not harmed" or to be kept "safe."

D is incorrect because "unharmed" does not mean "shy."

8

A is correct because Kress thinks about how the birds are in danger from too much hunting, meaning he was thinking about their safety.

B is incorrect because Kress says he "knew that puffins once lived in America," so he had prior knowledge about the birds.

C is incorrect because there is no way to know if Kress was on vacation or not based on the paragraph.

D is incorrect because while he is aware of puffins being hunted, there is nothing to indicate that Kress thinks he would never see the bird again; the sighting actually inspires him to help save the birds.

E is correct because Kress "was amazed" when he saw the puffins, showing that he was excited and interested in the birds.

9

Using the prefix *un-*, the word *unusual* means "not usual" or "strange." The word that uses *un-* in the same way is "untrue" or "not true."

10

A is incorrect because this detail is not in the passage.

B is correct because the author talks about the puffin's traits to show how the bird is so unique and distinctive.

C is incorrect because the author does not compare the puffin to other birds living in the same area.

D is incorrect because this detail is not in the passage.

11

A is incorrect because the word *was* does not rhyme with the word *went*.

B is incorrect because the word *like* does not rhyme with the word *went*.

C is incorrect because the word *flew* rhymes with the words *Peru* and *loopty-loo,* but not with the word *went*.

D is correct because the word *spent* rhymes with the word *went*.

12

A is incorrect because while the bird "tipped," it does not fall, so "like a plane" would not show the bird falling.

B is incorrect because "like a plane" does not show that the bird is the same length as a plane.

C is correct because "like a plane" shows how the bird "tipped" and moved gracefully.

D is incorrect because "like a plane" does not show that the bird is as heavy as the plane.

13

The poet repeats the soft *s* sound in *spring, sing,* and *softly.*

14A

A is correct because the speaker is someone who climbs the tree to see the cricket.

B is incorrect because the speaker talks about the cricket; it is not the cricket talking.

C is incorrect because the speaker would not be the tree based on the line, "Sing softly in your tree."

D is incorrect because the speaker uses the word *I* to describe what he or she does in the poem.

14B

A is incorrect because the line describes the cricket, not the speaker.

B is incorrect because the line is what the speaker imagines the cricket is saying, but it doesn't explain who the speaker is.

C is incorrect because the line describes the weather, not who the speaker of the poem is.

D is correct because the line is from the speaker as he or she is climbing up the tree to see the cricket.

15

A is incorrect because the meeting between the speaker and the cricket is quiet, not busy.

B is incorrect because the speaker does not talk about feeling tired when meeting the cricket.

C is correct because the simile is used to describe the lack of movement between the speaker and the cricket when they come face to face.

D is incorrect because the speaker does not feel scared meeting the cricket.

E is correct because the simile shows how the meeting between the speaker and cricket is calm.

16

A is incorrect because "Veronica" is a proper noun and should be capitalized.

B is correct because "Veronica's" is a possessive noun modifying "dog."

C is incorrect because "dog" is a common noun and should not be capitalized.

D is incorrect because an apostrophe is necessary to indicate that the dog belongs to Veronica.

17

A is incorrect because an apostrophe is necessary to indicate possession.

B is incorrect because there is an error with the spelling of the possessive noun.

C is incorrect because there is an error with the spelling of the possessive noun.

D is correct because the word *puppies'* is a plural possessive noun modifying "names."

18

A is incorrect because this creates a run-on sentence.

B is incorrect because a conjunction is missing, and the words do not create a concise meaning.

C is correct because the conjunction *and* correctly combines the predicate nouns.

D is incorrect because a conjunction is missing, and the words do not create a concise meaning.

19

A is correct because the plural possessive *their* indicates that "feet" should be used.

B is incorrect because there is a spelling error.

C is incorrect because there is a spelling error.

D is incorrect because the plural possessive *their* indicates that "feet" should be used, not "foot."

20

A is incorrect because there is a spelling error.

B is correct because the pronoun *several* indicates that the plural "families" should be used.

C is incorrect because there is a spelling error.

D is incorrect because the pronoun *several* indicates that the plural "families" should be used, not "family."

Unit 3 Answer Key

Student Name: _____

Question	Correct Answer	Content Focus	Complexity
1	B	Problem and Solution	DOK 2
2A	A	Problem and Solution	DOK 2
2B	B	Problem and Solution/ Text Evidence	DOK 2
3	D, E	Suffixes: -able	DOK 1
4	see below	Context Clues: Synonyms	DOK 2
5	C	Problem and Solution	DOK 2
6	B	Suffixes: -able	DOK 1
7	see below	Sequence	DOK 2
8	see below	Sequence	DOK 2
9	C	Suffixes: -ly	DOK 1
10A	A	Main Idea and Key Details	DOK 2
10B	D	Main Idea and Key Details/ Text Evidence	DOK 2
11A	C	Main Idea and Key Details	DOK 2
11B	B	Main Idea and Key Details/ Text Evidence	DOK 2
12	see below	Context Clues: Synonyms	DOK 2
13	A	Text Features: Key Words/Charts	DOK 2
14	B, D	Text Features: Charts	DOK 2
15	C	Suffixes: -y	DOK 1
16	A	Present-Tense Verbs	DOK 1
17	C	Combining Sentences with Verbs	DOK 1
18	B	Past-Tense Verbs	DOK 1
19	C	Action Verbs	DOK 1
20	D	Future-Tense Verbs	DOK 1

Comprehension 1, 2A, 2B, 5, 7, 8, 10A, 10B, 11A, 11B, 13, 14		/18	%
Vocabulary 3, 4, 6, 9, 12, 15		/12	%
English Language Conventions 16, 17, 18, 19, 20		/5	%
Total Unit 3 Assessment Score		/35	%

4 Students should circle the following word:

- asked

7 **2-point response:** The first section "Flies Come from Flies" explains a new experiment that Redi did. The section "More to Prove" explains that Redi's experiment only partly convinced people that living things come only from living things. There was more to prove. So "More to Prove" builds on the information in "Flies Come from Flies." It also shows the sequence of events by explaining that 200 years passed before Pasteur's experiment convinced people completely.

8 Students should put the events in the following order:

- First – Pasteur put soup broth into two bottles.
- Second – Pasteur boiled the soup broth.
- Third – Pasteur used a straight and a twisted tube for the bottle tops.
- Fourth – Pasteur found germs in the bottle with the straight tube top.

12 Students should circle the following words:

- look
- see

Opinion Performance Task			
Question	**Answer**	**Complexity**	**Score**
1	see below	DOK 2	/1
2	see below	DOK 3	/2
3	see below	DOK 3	/2
Article	see below	DOK 4	/4 [P/O] /4 [E/F] /2 [C]
Total Score			**/15**

1   • Animals' bodies help them in different ways.
       – Pandas have an extra thumb that helps them hold bamboo.
     • Some animals can be very hard to find.
       – Squid live in deep, dark places.

2   **2-point response:** Sources #1 and #2 show that the way people try to observe animals depends on the animal. Pandas live alone in the mountains. They are very shy. To watch them in the wild, people have to go to where they are and be very patient. For example, George Schaller spent years watching pandas in the woods, but he only got to see them 16 times. Since pandas also live in zoos and on reserves, there are other ways for people to study them, but people might not learn the same kinds of things about pandas.

3   **2-point response:** People observe animals in the wild because they can learn different things about them there. For example, Source #2 explains that George Schaller studied how much bamboo pandas eat in the wild. In a zoo, they might eat a different amount of bamboo since it is given to them. Source #1 explains that squid are hard to find at all because they live in deep water. By finding a way to watch them, people were able to learn that their skin changes colors.

10-point anchor paper: I think that giant squid are interesting animals because they are built differently than other sea animals. Giant squid are built in a way that helps them live in their environment. They are also able to do interesting things that help them live. The most special thing about squid is that they are able to live in a part of the ocean where many other sea animals do not live.

In order to live in the dark, deep waters they call home, giant squid have very large eyes, according to Source #1. These large eyes help them see even though there is not much light. This helps squid move around, find prey, and avoid danger. According to Source #1, they also have strong muscles, long tentacles, and sharp beaks. This helps them move quickly and catch prey. This may be especially important since fewer sea animals live in the deeper parts of the ocean where the giant squid live. Once people figured out how to watch giant squid in their ocean homes using video cameras, they learned that giant squid can change colors, according to Source #1. This may be to blend in or to scare or lure other animals. One thing is for sure; the giant squid are some of the most interesting animals there are.

I chose to write about the giant squid because the things that make them different from other animals also help them survive and make them really interesting. They have arms, tentacles, beaks, and the ability to change color. The giant squid are proof that being different can be good.

Copyright © McGraw-Hill Education

Unit 3 Rationales

1

A is incorrect because it isn't until the sixth paragraph that the nightingale's role is explained in the passage.

B is correct because the paragraph explains that the villagers are worried about who will replace the wise man.

C is incorrect because the young men are not mentioned until the third paragraph, and the reader does not learn how the men will be tested until later in the passage.

D is incorrect because the third paragraph explains how the wise man will test three young men from the village to determine who will replace him.

2A

A is correct because the villagers are worried about finding someone who will continue to help them with their problems.

B is incorrect because the nightingale doesn't really lose her way; she is part of the test for the men.

C is incorrect because this is not the main problem and is part of the test for the men.

D is incorrect because this is not a problem in the passage.

2B

A is incorrect because this is a detail describing the wise man's role, not the problem in the passage.

B is correct because this quote from the villagers supports the problem of finding a new wise man.

C is incorrect because this is a detail describing the test the wise man creates.

D is incorrect because this is a detail that does not support the problem in the passage.

3

A is incorrect because "cable" does not contain a root and a suffix.

B is incorrect because "table" does not contain the suffix -*able*.

C is incorrect because "stable" does not contain a root and the suffix -*able*.

D is correct because "fixable" contains the root *fix* and the suffix -*able*.

E is correct because "enjoyable" contains the root *joy* and the suffix -*able*.

4

The word *asked* should be circled because it is a synonym for "invited."

5

A is incorrect because the wise man does not pretend to be a nightingale in the passage.

B is incorrect because at the end of the passage the wise man chooses a new wise man for the village.

C is correct because the wise man uses the nightingale to see who of the three young men will respond correctly.

D is incorrect because although the wise man asks the villagers to send three clever men, they do not choose who will be the new wise man.

6

A is incorrect because the suffix *-able* means "capable of, tending to, or given to." It does not mean "after."

B is correct because "laughable" means "tending to laugh" or "ready to laugh."

C is incorrect because the suffix *-able* does not mean "before."

D is incorrect because the suffix *-able* does not mean "not."

7

See answer key for sample response.

8

First, Pasteur put soup broth into two bottles, which he subsequently boiled. Then he made shapes for the tops of the bottles. He used a straight tube and a twisted tube. In the end, he found germs in the bottle with the straight tube top, showing that it was easier for germs to enter the straight tube instead of the twisted tube.

9

A is incorrect because the suffix *-ly* means "like," so the word *tightly* means "tight-like," not broken.

B is incorrect because the word *tightly* does not mean the jar is clear.

C is correct because the word *tightly* means that the jar is firmly secured and hard to open.

D is incorrect because the word *tightly* does not mean the jar is filled to the top.

10A

A is correct because this sentence describes what the passage is about.

B is incorrect because this is not what occurs in the passage.

C is incorrect because this is a detail and not what the entire passage is about.

D is incorrect because this is not a detail in the passage.

10B

A is incorrect because this is a detail that does not support the main idea.

B is incorrect because this is a detail about only one scientist that does not support the main idea.

C is incorrect because this is a detail that does not support the main idea.

D is correct because this is a detail that supports the main idea of what Redi and Pasteur discovered.

11A

A is incorrect because the information about humus is a detail and not the main idea.

B is incorrect because this is a detail about farmers using soil for crops, not the main idea; it's also only mentioned at the end of the passage.

C is correct because the passage is about how soil is formed and its many purposes.

D is incorrect because this is a detail about rock breaking down, and soil is not specified in the sentence.

11B

A is incorrect because this is a sentence that supports the detail that soil has many different living things.

B is correct because the main idea of the passage is that soil is formed when rock gets weathered and then is mixed with decaying living things.

C is incorrect because this related detail discusses one part of the weathering process.

D is incorrect because this detail discusses a related idea that soil has different layers.

12

The words *look* and *see* have almost the same meaning as "observed."

13

A is correct because the title and words *layers of soil* tell that the chart will be about just that.

B is incorrect because the chart is not just about what the soil has but also what characteristics each layer has.

C is incorrect because the words help show a detail about a layer but not what the whole chart is about.

D is incorrect because the words help show what a layer has but not what the whole chart is about.

14

A is incorrect because plants are living things and being in a layer with no living things would not help plants grow.

B is correct because the chart says Layer A is dark in color, which is a healthy color for growing plants.

C is incorrect because a plant has roots in order to grow and not having any roots will not help the plants grow.

D is correct because plants need water to grow and this layer holds water easily, which should help the plants grow.

E is incorrect because the chart says Layer B has bits of rock, not Layer A.

15

A is incorrect because the suffix *-y* means "characterized by," not "look like."

B is incorrect because the suffix *-y* means "characterized by," not "without."

C is correct because the suffix *-y* means "characterized by," so the word *sandy* means "characterized by or having sand."

D is incorrect because the suffix *-y* means "characterized by," not "in need of."

16

A is correct because the sentence contains the present-tense verb *writes*.

B is incorrect because the sentence does not contain a present-tense verb.

C is incorrect because the sentence does not contain a present-tense verb.

D is incorrect because the sentence does not contain a present-tense verb.

17

A is incorrect because the sentence is a comma splice.

B is incorrect because the sentence is missing a conjunction and a subject.

C is correct because the conjunction *and* correctly joins the two clauses.

D is incorrect because the sentence is missing information and changes the meaning of the sentences.

18

A is incorrect because the sentence does not contain a past-tense verb.

B is correct because the sentence contains the past-tense verb *felt*.

C is incorrect because the sentence does not contain a past-tense verb.

D is incorrect because the sentence does not contain a past-tense verb.

19

A is incorrect because the sentence does not contain an action verb.

B is incorrect because the sentence does not contain an action verb.

C is correct because the sentence contains the action verb *saw*.

D is incorrect because the sentence does not contain an action verb.

20

A is incorrect because the sentence does not contain a future-tense verb.

B is incorrect because the sentence does not contain a future-tense verb.

C is incorrect because the sentence does not contain a future-tense verb.

D is correct because the sentence contains the future-tense verb *will be*.

Unit 4 Answer Key

Student Name: _____

Question	Correct Answer	Content Focus	Complexity
1A	C	Point of View	DOK 2
1B	C	Point of View/ Text Evidence	DOK 2
2	B	Metaphor	DOK 2
3	see below	Theme	DOK 3
4	see below	Sentence Clues	DOK 2
5	A, E	Literary Elements: Illustrations	DOK 2
6	A, B	Sentence Clues	DOK 2
7	see below	Text Structure: Compare and Contrast	DOK 2
8A	D	Text Structure: Compare and Contrast	DOK 2
8B	C	Text Structure: Compare and Contrast/ Text Evidence	DOK 2
9	B	Text Features: Captions	DOK 2
10	A	Prefixes: *im-*	DOK 1
11	B	Point of View	DOK 2
12A	C	Theme	DOK 3
12B	A	Theme/ Text Evidence	DOK 3
13	C, E	Metaphor	DOK 2
14	see below	Point of View	DOK 2
15	A	Sentence Clues	DOK 2
16	D	Linking Verbs	DOK 1
17	A	Irregular Verbs	DOK 1
18	C	Main and Helping Verbs	DOK 1
19	A	Irregular Verbs	DOK 1
20	B	Linking Verbs	DOK 1

Comprehension 1A, 1B, 3, 5, 7, 8A, 8B, 9, 11, 12A, 12B, 14	/18	%
Vocabulary 2, 4, 6, 10, 13, 15	/12	%
English Language Conventions 16, 17, 18, 19, 20	/5	%
Total Unit 4 Assessment Score	/35	%

3   **2-point response:** In this passage, Carmen, the main character, learns that if she doesn't give up in difficult situations, she could end up having wonderful experiences. At one point in the passage, Carmen is so nervous about learning her lines for the play that she decides to quit. Luckily, her family convinces her not to give up. Even though she is still scared, she finds a solution and gets through the play. At the end of the passage, Carmen is happy, and her parents are proud because she didn't give up.

4   Students should circle the following word:
  • tell

7   Students should match the following:
  • Whales—live in the ocean
  • Other Mammals—have hair or fur
  • Both—feed their babies milk

14 Students should underline the following line:
  • "But much more than that, I'm just glad he's my dad."

Unit 4 Answer Key

Student Name: _____

Narrative Performance Task			
Question	Answer	Complexity	Score
1	see below	DOK 2	/1
2	see below	DOK 3	/2
3	see below	DOK 3	/2
Story	see below	DOK 4	/4 [P/O] /4 [D/E] /2 [C]
Total Score			/15

1   • Source #1: Desert Heroes
    - Some desert animals can stay protected during sandstorms.
    • Source #2: The Big-Eared Fox
    - Some desert animals can cool down in ways besides sweating.
    • Both Source #1 and Source #2
    - Some desert animals can go days without drinking water.

2   **2-point response:** It is important that the camel and fennec fox have bodies that can handle temperature changes. Source #1 says the camel's body handles hot days because of the coolness that it stores during cold nights. This is important because it shows that the camel's body is made to handle changing temperatures. Source #2 says the fennec fox handles changing temperatures by using its fur as protection. During the day, the fox's fur protects it from the sun's heat. During cold nights, the fox's fur keeps it warm. This is important because no matter the temperature, the fennec fox is protected.

3   **2-point response:** These animals' feet help them live in the desert because of the special way that their feet are made. Source #1 says that a camel's feet spread out like snowshoes when it walks. Because its feet spread out, the camel does not sink into the sand when it walks. Source #2 says that the fennec fox's feet are good shovels because of the way that they are made. This is helpful to the fox because having feet like this helps it dig the underground dens that it sleeps in during the day.

10-point anchor paper: Nadia and her family were visiting relatives in Morocco. She had never visited the country before and felt so amazed by everything she saw. The food, clothing, and nature were beautiful! She had never seen so many wonderful patterns and colors before in her life. She also made so many friends. But Nadia was most excited for the adventure that awaited them on their last weekend there. Nadia and her family were going to ride camels in the Sahara Desert!

Nadia had learned about camels in school. She knew that they were built perfectly for the desert because they don't need a lot of water. Their eyes keep sand away, and their lips help them eat plants. They drink a lot of water when they find it and keep it stored for later. Their feet also protect them from the hot sand. This helps the camel travel for a long time. Nadia was so excited to see a real camel up close!

Nadia and her family started their trip early in the morning before it became too hot. They took a bus to the edge of the desert and met their guide. He welcomed them and told lots of funny jokes. Then they saw the camels. Nadia was surprised at how much bigger they were than she expected! The guide helped her get on top of the camel. Nadia became a little scared once she saw how high up she was. She was worried she wouldn't be able to do the trip after all.

Nadia saw her mom looking at her. Nadia told her how she was feeling. "Don't worry. Lots of people go on these trips, and they have an amazing time. You are in responsible hands," Nadia's mom told her. Nadia felt a little better. Once everyone was on top of their camels, they slowly made their way deeper into the desert. Once they were moving, Nadia was amazed by all the shimmering colors. She completely forgot about how scared she was feeling earlier. She couldn't wait to tell all her friends back home about the fact that she rode a camel. She was so happy her family was with her on this adventure!

Unit 4 Rationales

1A

A is incorrect because this detail does not reveal how Carmen's parents felt about her performance.

B is incorrect because this detail is not in the passage.

C is correct because Carmen's parents clap loudly, showing that they feel excited and proud of her.

D is incorrect because this detail is not in the passage.

1B

A is incorrect because this sentence does not support how Carmen's parents feel about her performance; her father tries to reassure her about the play.

B is incorrect because this sentence does not support how Carmen's parents feel about her performance.

C is correct because Carmen's parents cheer and applaud after her performance, showing they are proud of her.

D is incorrect because Carmen's parents going backstage does not help to show their feelings.

2

A is incorrect because there is no evidence that being "a bundle of nerves" has to do with carrying lots of things.

B is correct because there is evidence showing that Carmen "could not stop worrying" and being "a bundle of nerves" means that she feels scared about performing.

C is incorrect because there is no evidence that Carmen needs help with her costumes.

D is incorrect because Carmen never says anything about the stage not looking good.

3

See answer key for sample response.

4

The word *tell* should be circled because it helps the student figure out the meaning of "announced."

5

A is correct because the illustration shows people laughing and having a good time, proving that Carmen does a great job.

B is incorrect because the illustration does not show Carmen preparing for the play; she is in the middle of the play.

C is incorrect because Carmen does not use the newspaper at all in the illustration.

D is incorrect because Carmen does not look nervous in the illustration.

E is correct because Carmen is smiling and strutting on stage, showing that she feels confident and relaxed.

F is incorrect because every seat is occupied by a person in the illustration.

6

A is correct because "break out strongly" is a way to describe a whale bursting out of the water.

B is correct because "jump up suddenly" is a way to describe a whale bursting out of the water.

C is incorrect because "swim away quickly" is not a way to describe a whale bursting out of the water.

D is incorrect because "hide slowly" is not a way to describe a whale bursting out of the water.

E is incorrect because "clap loudly" is not a way to describe a whale bursting out of the water.

7

The passage describes how whales live in the ocean. It also explains that all mammals except whales have hair or fur. However, both feed their babies milk.

8A

A is incorrect because both humans and whales breathe using lungs.

B is incorrect because both humans and whales raise their babies.

C is incorrect because both humans and whales communicate with each other.

D is correct because the passage explains that whales can hold their breath for a long time, which is something humans cannot do.

8B

A is incorrect because this sentence does not support any detail from Part A showing the difference between whales and humans.

B is incorrect because this sentence does not support any detail from Part A showing the difference between whales and humans.

C is correct because whales holding their breath for an hour is something humans cannot do and supports the main difference between whales and humans.

D is incorrect because this sentence does not support any detail from Part A showing the difference between whales and humans.

9

A is incorrect because the caption doesn't mention anything about where whales go.

B is correct because the caption describes adult humpback whales as being 50 to 60 feet long.

C is incorrect because the caption doesn't mention anything about the noises whales make.

D is incorrect because the caption doesn't mention anything about the weight of the whales.

10

A is correct because the prefix *im-* means "not" or "not developed."

B is incorrect because the prefix *im-* does not mean "fully."

C is incorrect because the prefix *im-* does not mean "quickly."

D is incorrect because the prefix *im-* does not mean "almost."

11

A is incorrect because while the dad might be a good grader, this is not what the narrator thinks is cool about him.

B is correct because the poem is about how the dad helps his students, which the narrator sees as being "cool."

C is incorrect because this detail is not in the poem.

D is incorrect because this detail is not in the poem.

12A

A is incorrect because not having enough money for a gift is a detail in the poem and not the main lesson.

B is incorrect because this is not a main lesson of the poem.

C is correct because the poem is all about how the dad works hard to help his students.

D is incorrect because this is a detail in the poem and not part of the main lesson.

12B

A is correct because the dad will work hard to help his students, which is a great thing to do.

B is incorrect because this detail does not support the main lesson of the poem.

C is incorrect because this detail does not support the main lesson of the poem.

D is incorrect because this detail does not support the main lesson of the poem.

13

A is incorrect because the metaphor is not meant to be taken literally.

B is incorrect because the metaphor is not meant to be taken literally.

C is correct because the dad seems like a knight who wants to help those students in trouble.

D is incorrect because the metaphor has nothing to do with the way the dad dresses.

E is correct because the dad seems like a knight who wants to help those students in trouble.

14

The line "But much more than that, I'm just glad he's my dad" shows that the speaker feels happy and proud of his or her father.

15

A is correct because "distinguish" is used to show how the student needs glasses in order to see clearly.

B is incorrect because "distinguish" does not refer to a specific person.

C is incorrect because "distinguish" is not about seeing something as the same.

D is incorrect because "distinguish" does not refer to a specific person.

16

A is incorrect because this would cause an error in verb tense.

B is incorrect because using "are" would cause an error in subject-verb agreement.

C is incorrect because a present participle has no place in the sentence.

D is correct because the past-tense "was" is the correct linking verb for this sentence.

17

A is correct because the past-tense "had" is the correct form to use in the sentence.

B is incorrect because "haved" is not the past tense of the irregular verb *have*.

C is incorrect because using "have" would cause an error in subject-verb agreement.

D is incorrect because this would cause an error in verb tense.

18

A is incorrect because the helping verb is missing here.

B is incorrect because the helping verb *are* does not work in this sentence.

C is correct because "were" is the correct helping verb to use with the main verb *calling*.

D is incorrect because the helping verb *will be* does not work in this sentence.

19

A is correct because "won" is the correct form of the irregular verb *win* to use in the sentence.

B is incorrect because this would cause an error in verb tense.

C is incorrect because the irregular verb *win* is not used in this way.

D is incorrect because the irregular verb *win* is not used in this way.

20

A is incorrect because this would cause an error in verb tense.

B is correct because "is" is the correct linking verb to use in the sentence.

C is incorrect because using "were" would cause an error in subject-verb agreement.

D is incorrect because this would cause an error in verb tense.

Unit 5 Answer Key

Student Name: _____

Question	Correct Answer	Content Focus	Complexity
1A	A	Point of View	DOK 2
1B	C	Point of View/ Text Evidence	DOK 2
2	see below	Point of View	DOK 2
3	C, E	Prefixes and Suffixes	DOK 1
4	see below	Point of View	DOK 2
5	B	Context Clues: Homophones	DOK 1
6A	C	Cause and Effect	DOK 2
6B	A	Cause and Effect/ Text Evidence	DOK 2
7	see below	Cause and Effect	DOK 2
8	B	Root Words	DOK 1
9	A	Context Clues: Homophones	DOK 1
10	D	Text Features: Timelines	DOK 2
11A	B	Author's Point of View	DOK 3
11B	C	Author's Point of View/ Text Evidence	DOK 3
12	B	Prefixes and Suffixes	DOK 1
13	see below	Author's Point of View	DOK 3
14	A	Text Features: Captions	DOK 2
15	C, D	Root Words	DOK 1
16	C	Possessive Pronouns	DOK 1
17	B	Pronoun-Verb Agreement	DOK 1
18	A	Pronoun-Verb Agreement	DOK 1
19	C	Subject and Object Pronouns	DOK 1
20	D	Pronoun-Verb Contractions	DOK 1

Comprehension 1A, 1B, 2, 4, 6A, 6B, 7, 10, 11A, 11B, 13, 14	/18	%
Vocabulary 3, 5, 8, 9, 12, 15	/12	%
English Language Conventions 16, 17, 18, 19, 20	/5	%
Total Unit 5 Assessment Score	/35	%

2   Students should circle the following options:
- Blank 1 — unkind
- Blank 2 — silly

4   **2-point response:** The brothers' view of the plan at the beginning of the passage is that it is too dangerous. They think the troll will hurt them and that they have no chance of succeeding. However, the brothers' view of the plan at the end is that it is very smart. They trick the troll and have another meadow to feed from.

7   Students should match the following:
- Cause 1— Effect: Marconi runs tests sending wireless signals a mile away.
- Cause 2— Effect: Marconi sends wireless signals from England to Canada.

13   Students should circle the following sentences:
- "Children need to have it in their lives."
- "School officials would be wise to require students to play an instrument starting in second grade."

Student Name: _____

Informational Performance Task			
Question	Answer	Complexity	Score
1	B, F	DOK 2	/1
2	see below	DOK 3	/2
3	see below	DOK 3	/2
Article	see below	DOK 4	/4 [P/O] /4 [E/E] /2 [C]
Total Score			/15

2   **2-point response:** In both sources people took action by doing something to protect the land. Source #1 says that the farmers protected the land by using trees to stop the wind from blowing away loose soil. Source #2 says that people protected the forests by using the Smokey the Bear character to teach people how to protect forests from fires.

3   **2-point response:** This topic is important because taking action helps protect people and animals. Source #1 says the farmers had to take action by protecting the soil from washing or blowing away. This is important because if there was no soil on farms, then certain crops could not grow. Source #2 says it was important for people to take action because without something to remind people to prevent forest fires, then more of the forest might burn down. More fires would hurt both people and the animals that depend on the forest to survive.

10-point anchor paper: People take action when they want to see change happen. Usually, people are either not happy with the ways things are at the time or they want to make sure that things do not get worse. There is usually a reason for people to take action. A reason may be that they want to protect what they currently have. An example of this is farmers who want to protect the soil on their farms from being destroyed by wind and water. The farmers are not happy with the soil on their farms being destroyed, so they take action to make sure that the soil is not harmed. Another reason people may take action is because they want to make sure that the situation does not get worse over time. An example of this is people who take action to protect forests from fire. Since the forests are homes to many types of trees, plants, and animals, it is important that the forests be protected.

The ways that people take action depends on what caused them to want to see the change happen. If something is happening that people are not happy with, then they will take action by making sure that the cause of the problem stops. Farmers who want to protect the soil on their farms take action by making sure that wind and water do not take away the soil. The farmers use different ways to stop the soil from being destroyed. They may plant trees next to a field so that the trees keep the wind from blowing away the soil. Farmers also take action by growing the kinds of plants with roots that will keep the soil in place. Lastly, farmers will make sure that the soil on their farms is strong. They will take action to do this by not planting anything in the soil for one growing season. During this time, farmers will only add non-living plant and animal parts to the soil so that the soil will be rich for the next growing season.

Other ways people take action is by making sure that the situation does not get worse or that it gets better over time. Since forests are important to both people and animals, it is important that they be protected from fires. People took action seventy years ago to make sure that forests were protected from fire by introducing the Smokey the Bear character. Smokey the Bear is used to teach people how to protect forests from fires. By putting signs in the forests, people are reminded to be careful and not do things that might cause a forest fire.

Because people take action, things change or get better. Farmers take action to protect soil and make sure it is not washed away. They also make sure the soil on their farms becomes stronger. Without strong soil, the food that Americans eat would not be able to grow. The effect of people taking action to protect forests from fire is that people know more about what to do to keep fires from starting. Since over half of forest fires are started by people, it is important that people know what they can do to keep forest fires from happening. With fewer fires, forests are protected and people and animals can continue to gain from the many different things that nature gives.

Unit 5 Rationales

1A

A is correct because Bill and Bo think Biff has a clever plan that they try to execute.

B is incorrect because there is no evidence in the passage that the brothers think Biff is selfish.

C is incorrect because there is no evidence in the passage that the brothers think Biff is foolish.

D is incorrect because there is no evidence in the passage that the brothers think Biff is funny.

1B

A is incorrect because this is a detail about the goats trying to find food; it does not support how Bill and Bo view Biff.

B is incorrect because this is a detail about the troll being scary; it does not support how Bill and Bo view Biff.

C is correct because Bill and Bo view Biff as clever for coming up with a crafty plan to get over the bridge.

D is incorrect because this is a detail about the troll trying to stop the goats; it does not support how Bill and Bo view Biff.

2

The three billy goats think that the troll is mean or unkind. Meanwhile, the troll thinks the goats are silly for even attempting to cross the bridge.

3

A is incorrect because "disagree" means to "not agree" or to not approve of something; it does not mean "to be alike."

B is incorrect because "disagree" does not indicate getting along with someone.

C is correct because "disagree" means to not approve or to oppose.

D is incorrect because "disagree" does not mean "to understand each other."

E is correct because "disagree" means to not approve or to have a different opinion on something.

4

See answer key for sample response.

5

A is incorrect because "home" and "here" do not have the same pronunciation.

B is correct because "hear" and "here" have the same pronunciation but different spellings and meanings.

C is incorrect because while "hair" and "here" might sound similar, they ultimately have different pronunciations.

D is incorrect because "hurry" and "here" do not have the same pronunciation.

6A

A is incorrect because Morse code was already invented.

B is incorrect because nothing in the passage suggests that people did not travel that far at that time.

C is correct because people could not send messages wirelessly at that time, so their messages could not cross the ocean.

D is incorrect because the passage indicates that people did have electricity at that time.

6B

A is correct because the sentence supports why people couldn't send messages wirelessly across the Atlantic Ocean.

B is incorrect because this detail does not explain why messages couldn't be sent far away.

C is incorrect because this detail is shown much later in the passage after wireless telegraphy becomes popular.

D is incorrect because this detail is shown much later in the passage after wireless telegraphy becomes popular.

7

The first cause-and-effect relationship explains how Marconi ran tests with wireless signals because he knew that radio waves carry electric signals through the air.

The second cause-and-effect relationship explains that Marconi sent wireless signals from England to Canada to prove that scientists were wrong in believing that radio waves could not travel far.

8

A is incorrect because "vent" is not the root word of "invention."

B is correct because the word *invent,* meaning to make something, is the root word of "invention."

C is incorrect because the suffix *-tion* is not the root word of "invention."

D is incorrect because "inve" is not the root word of "invention."

9

A is correct because the context clues indicate that Marconi was the only person who could make or sell his product.

B is incorrect because this is the meaning of the homophone *rite.*

C is incorrect because the context clues do not support this meaning of the homophone *right.*

D is incorrect because this is the meaning of the homophone *write.*

10

A is incorrect because the timeline does not tell about places where Marconi lived.

B is incorrect because the timeline does not show how Marconi's work led to Morse code.

C is incorrect because the timeline does not help the reader determine how Marconi came up with his invention.

D is correct because the timeline shows major events in Marconi's life in the order in which they occurred.

11A

A is incorrect because the author does not compare playing music to other activities.

B is correct because the author explains that playing music helps students learn different skills at once.

C is incorrect because the author says that playing music "makes you want to dance" but does not discuss students dancing during school.

D is incorrect because the author explains that learning to play music is a way to use math, but the author does not give the opinion that it is the only way.

11B

A is incorrect because the sentence does not help support the author's point of view about learning skills by playing music.

B is incorrect because the sentence does not help support the author's point of view about learning skills by playing music.

C is correct because this sentence supports the author's point of view that playing music lets you learn lots of different things.

D is incorrect because the author stresses that music helps people gain different skills, not just math skills.

12

A is incorrect because the suffix *-able* does not mean "without."

B is correct because the suffix *-able* means "able to be" or "can be," so the word *valuable* means "can be valued."

C is incorrect because the suffix *-able* does not mean "waiting to have."

D is incorrect because the suffix *-able* does not mean "sometimes."

13

Students should circle the sentence that states the opinion that children "need" to have music and the sentence that includes the word *wise*:

"Children need to have it in their lives."

"School officials would be wise to require students to play an instrument starting in second grade."

14

A is correct because the caption under the photo of the sheet music includes information about how music improves the memory.

B is incorrect because while the song shown may be fun to sing, the caption is not about that.

C is incorrect because it doesn't talk about how sheet music is confusing.

D is incorrect because while the caption does talk about exercise, it's not about regular exercise.

15

A is incorrect because the root word of *creative* is "create," which does not mean "control."

B is incorrect because the root word of *creative* is "create," which does not mean "forget."

C is correct because the root word of *creative* is "create," which means "make."

D is correct because the root word of *creative* is "create," which means "build."

E is incorrect because the root word of *creative* is "create," which does not mean "sell."

16

A is incorrect because the objective pronoun *us* does not make sense in the sentence.

B is incorrect because the town is a single entity and does not require the plural *ours*.

C is correct because the possessive pronoun *our* is needed in the sentence.

D is incorrect because the personal pronoun *them* does not make sense in the sentence.

17

A is incorrect because this creates an error in the pronoun-verb agreement.

B is correct because the verb *lives* agrees with the pronoun *he* in the sentence.

C is incorrect because the present participle *living* does not belong in this sentence.

D is incorrect because this tense does not make sense in the context of the sentence.

18

A is correct because the verb *have* agrees with the pronoun *I* in the sentence.

B is incorrect because this creates an error in pronoun-verb agreement.

C is incorrect because the present participle *having* does not belong in this sentence.

D is incorrect because "haved" is not the past-tense form of the irregular verb *have*.

19

A is incorrect because the objective pronoun *them* does not belong in the sentence.

B is incorrect because the possessive *their* does not belong in the sentence.

C is correct because the subjective pronoun *they* refers to the clothes mentioned in the previous sentence.

D is incorrect because the contraction *they're* does not belong in the sentence.

20

A is incorrect because "they's" is not a contraction that is ever formed due to the error in subject-verb agreement.

B is incorrect because the apostrophe is missing in the contraction.

C is incorrect because the objective pronoun *them* does not belong in the sentence.

D is correct because the pronoun-verb contraction *they've* refers to the neighbors in the sentence.

Unit 6 Answer Key

Student Name: _____

Question	Correct Answer	Content Focus	Complexity
1	C	Stage Directions	DOK 2
2	see below	Theme	DOK 3
3A	B	Point of View	DOK 2
3B	A	Point of View/ Text Evidence	DOK 2
4	D	Idioms	DOK 2
5	C	Idioms	DOK 2
6	A	Problem and Solution	DOK 2
7	B	Greek and Latin Roots	DOK 1
8A	C	Problem and Solution	DOK 2
8B	D	Problem and Solution/ Text Evidence	DOK 2
9	see below	Problem and Solution	DOK 2
10	C, E	Root Words	DOK 1
11	B, E	Point of View	DOK 2
12	see below	Idioms	DOK 2
13A	A	Theme	DOK 3
13B	D	Theme/ Text Evidence	DOK 3
14	see below	Point of View	DOK 2
15	C	Greek and Latin Roots	DOK 1
16	B	Prepositions	DOK 1
17	D	Adverbs that Compare	DOK 1
18	A	Adjectives that Compare	DOK 1
19	C	Prepositions	DOK 1
20	B	Adjectives and Articles	DOK 1

Comprehension 1, 2, 3A, 3B, 6, 8A, 8B, 9, 11, 13A, 13B, 14	/18	%
Vocabulary 4, 5, 7, 10, 12, 15	/12	%
English Language Conventions 16, 17, 18, 19, 20	/5	%
Total Unit 6 Assessment Score	/35	%

2   Students should underline the following lines:
  - "I should have listened to you."
  - "He realizes too late that he should have heeded his father's advice."

9   Students should match the following:
  - Problem- Many animals and plants are dying off.
  - Solution- People can learn to care about nature.

12   Students should circle the following word:
  - joked

14   **2-point response:** The narrator thinks the eclipse is wonderful and feels glad to have seen it. The narrator shows these feelings with lines in the poem like, "How strange it was to think that Earth / Could block off all that light," and "I felt / so glad to be a part of this big crowd cheering for the moon." Later, on the train, the narrator keeps looking at the moon, which also helps to show that the event had a strong effect.

Student Name: _____

Opinion Performance Task			
Question	Answer	Complexity	Score
1	C, E	DOK 2	/1
2	see below	DOK 3	/2
3	see below	DOK 3	/2
Paper	see below	DOK 4	/4 [P/O] /4 [E/E] /2 [C]
Total Score			/15

2   **2-point response:** People can save what is important to them by putting in the time and effort that it takes to save important items. Source #2 says that people can save important items by creating a shadow box that can be kept on a bookshelf. They can also put together a scrapbook of important objects like photos or tickets, or they can make a quilt using old pieces of their favorite clothing. In the presentation, it says that people can save what is important by putting everyday objects like toys, tools, and letters into a container and burying the container to be opened at a later time.

3   **2-point response:** People save what is important to them because they get some type of reward from what it is that they are saving. Source #1 says that people may choose to save libraries because of all that they offer the community such as tutoring and book clubs. The source, *Time Capsules,* says that people may choose to create a time capsule as a way to share with future generations what was important at the time that the capsule was created.

10-point anchor paper: People are always saying how important it is to try new things, so why would someone want to save items from the past? The past already happened so the items from the past should stay in the past. I disagree that it is important to save items from the past.

Because things change, there is no point in keeping items from the past. Things change and people have to keep up with this change. For example, libraries will become unnecessary due to the way technology has changed. People do not have to go the library anymore to get books because they can download them from the Internet. There is no point in saving a library when the community can receive the services that a library offers in other ways. If someone needs help with research, then he or she does not have to ask a librarian for help. He or she can ask a teacher at school or find the answer on the Internet. If someone is looking for a quiet place to study then there are plenty of other quiet places where the person can go, such as a park or classroom. Many libraries are closing because they do not have the money to stay open anymore. It would be better to use the money in other ways, such as making sure that everyone has access to the Internet, instead of making people use a place that is not so important now.

Saving items from the past can take a lot of effort and time. It can be expensive also. If saving photos, for example, someone has to take the photos using a camera and then there has to be a way to print and keep the photos so that they can be looked at later. Some people choose to use even more difficult ways to save items from the past, such as creating shadow boxes of important items, creating a scrapbook of events, or making quilts from their favorite clothes. Each of these ways of saving items requires equipment and materials. They also require a lot of time and effort that could be used in other ways. The best way to save something that is important is to keep a memory of it in your brain. A memory is more personal than an object because it is created by the person who is doing the remembering. Keeping an item in a wooden box or in a scrapbook does not show the feelings that went along with the event. However, if someone is sharing something from their memory, then that person can also share the feelings and excitement of that event. Instead of saving objects from the past, it would be better to talk about your favorite memory with your friends and family.

In my opinion, there is no point in saving items from the past. Items from the past are not useful for the present. Also, saving items from the past requires time, effort, and money that can be used in other ways. We cannot change what was important back then. Instead we should use our time and energy to make the present better by talking to each other and using our voices for change.

Unit 6 Rationales

1

A is incorrect because the stage directions do not use suspenseful language.

B is incorrect because the stage directions do not add humor.

C is correct because the stage directions explain that Icarus is the son of Daedalus.

D is incorrect because the stage directions only introduce Icarus; they do not explain what he or the other characters are thinking.

2

These two lines from the play support the theme of listening to a parent's instructions or advice:

"I should have listened to you."

"He realizes too late that he should have heeded his father's advice."

3A

A is incorrect because a play about Theseus would not be able to explain why Icarus stayed on the island.

B is correct because a play from Theseus's point of view would most likely include details between Theseus and Daedalus about Theseus's escape.

C is incorrect because this information would not be available to Theseus.

D is incorrect because knowing Theseus's point of view would not help explain how Icarus was caught and brought to the castle.

3B

A is correct because the detail highlights Daedalus helping Theseus escape for some reason that would be made clearer if it was told from Theseus's point of view.

B is incorrect because the detail is from Daedalus and doesn't mention Theseus escaping.

C is incorrect because the detail is from King Minos and doesn't mention Theseus escaping.

D is incorrect because the detail is from Icarus and doesn't mention Theseus escaping.

4

A is incorrect because Daedalus has just told the king his feelings about his son.

B is incorrect because Daedalus' feelings toward Icarus have yet to be revealed.

C is incorrect because Daedalus does not appear to be in a hurry to get away from the king.

D is correct because the idiom shows that Daedalus' pleading will not change the king's mind.

5

A is incorrect because the idiom "hit the nail on the head" does not mean "to miss a chance."

B is incorrect because the idiom "hit the nail on the head" does not mean "to work very hard."

C is correct because the idiom "hit the nail on the head" means "to say something exactly right"; Icarus said they would need wings, which are exactly what Daedalus built.

D is incorrect because the idiom "hit the nail on the head" does not mean "to believe someone without proof."

6

A is correct because the passage explains that Wilson had to do something else and "began watching ants."

B is incorrect because there is no evidence that Wilson went to different doctors.

C is incorrect because there is no evidence that Wilson wrote books on birds.

D is incorrect because there is no evidence that Wilson spent most of his time staying home.

7

A is incorrect because "inspect" does not necessarily mean that something must be done quickly.

B is correct because "inspect" means to look at something in a careful way.

C is incorrect because "inspect" does not only relate to change; something can be inspected even if it's not changing.

D is incorrect because "inspect" does not necessarily mean that something must be done for a long time.

8A

A is incorrect because only soldier ants fight other ants, and it's not a way to know that something dangerous is happening.

B is incorrect because ants will only stroke the belly of an aphid to get honeydew to eat.

C is correct because the following evidence is in the passage: "when one ant senses danger, it gives off an odor. The other ants smell it and make the same odor... Then they can hide or run away."

D is incorrect because there is no evidence that ants hide when they are being watched.

8B

A is incorrect because this is a detail about Wilson watching ants and doesn't say anything about danger.

B is incorrect because this is a detail about soldier ants specifically and doesn't say anything about ants detecting danger.

C is incorrect because this is a detail about getting honeydew from aphids.

D is correct because this sentence supports the idea that ants can smell an odor that tells them there's danger ahead.

9

A problem in the passage is that many animals and plants are dying off. However, the solution is to help people learn more about nature so that they want to conserve it.

10

A is incorrect because the root word of "collected" does not mean "try."

B is incorrect because the root word of "collected" does not mean "eat."

C is correct because the root word of "collected" is "collect," which means to "get or gather."

D is incorrect because the root word of "collected" does not mean "make."

E is correct because the root word of "collected" is "collect," which means to "get or gather."

11

A is incorrect because the narrator specifically mentions his or her legs falling asleep and not a general "unhealthy" feeling.

B is correct because the narrator mentions his or her legs had gone to sleep, encouraging movement.

C is incorrect because the narrator and Luis are playing computer games and not working hard at all.

D is incorrect because the narrator never mentions anything about falling asleep at the computer.

E is correct because the narrator talks about having to move because he or she hasn't been active all day.

12

The word *joked* helps to show that "pulling your leg" means acting silly and having fun.

13A

A is correct because the narrator realizes that staying home all day and not going outside would have caused him or her to miss the amazing eclipse.

B is incorrect because while the characters may dance in the poem, this is not the main theme.

C is incorrect because the poem is about a lunar eclipse and not the specific brightness of the moon.

D is incorrect because the eclipse helps to support a larger theme about adventure, not how often it occurs.

13B

A is incorrect because this is a detail about the eclipse.

B is incorrect because this is a detail about what happens during an eclipse.

C is incorrect because this is a detail about the characters having fun.

D is correct because this sentence supports the theme of finding excitement when you go outside.

14

See answer key for sample response.

15

A is incorrect because "astronaut" does not have anything to do with a pirate ship.

B is incorrect because "astronaut" does not refer only to a star.

C is correct because "astronaut" means a person who has been to space in a spacecraft.

D is incorrect because "astronaut" involves space, not studying ships.

16

A is incorrect because the sidewalk heat is not coming from the characters' feet.

B is correct because "under" is the best preposition to use in relation to "sidewalk."

C is incorrect because the sidewalk is not a separate entity from the characters' feet.

D is incorrect because the characters' feet are not in the sidewalk.

17

A is incorrect because "fast" does not compare the two actions described in the sentence.

B is incorrect because "fasts" does not compare the two actions described in the sentence.

C is incorrect because the superlative form is not needed here.

D is correct because the comparative form is needed here.

18

A is correct because the comparative adjective is needed here.

B is incorrect because the superlative adjective is not needed here.

C is incorrect because "sweaty" does not compare the two characters in the sentence.

D is incorrect because "sweat" does not compare the two characters in the sentence.

19

A is incorrect because "during" is used in relation to time, not location.

B is incorrect because "over" does not make sense within the context of the sentence.

C is correct because "to" is the best preposition to use in relation to "avenue."

D is incorrect because "for" does not make sense within the context of the sentence.

20

A is incorrect because the plural *these* does not agree with "food."

B is correct because the singular *this* agrees with "food" to show proximity.

C is incorrect because the plural *those* does not agree with "food."

D is incorrect because the personal pronoun *them* does not agree with "food."